Inklings On Philosophy & Theology

4th Edition

Revised and Abridged

Matthew Dominguez

By Matthew Dominguez

First printing September 2000
Nineteenth printing May 2019 – Revised and Abridged 4th Edition

WheatonPress.com
ISBN-13: 978-1-950258-12-3 (WheatonPress.com)
ISBN-10: 1-950258-12-2

This title is available at Amazon.com or wherever fine books are sold. Please visit the publisher online at www.WheatonPress.com for more books in this series, classroom or small group discounts, and other resources designed to equip you in your discipleship journey.

DEDICATION

For my students: *"A thousand thanks."*

For my future students: *"To the Breach!"*

To all of my family and friends
who have helped make the impossible, possible:
"Here's to water walking!"

To the next generation of water walkers:
"Further up and Further in!"

CONTENTS

SPECIAL THANKS

"It is not often that someone comes along who is a true friend and a good writer."
E. B. White, Charlotte's Web

This book would literally not exist without the massive encouragement, support, expertise, and sacrifice of so many people, the first of whom is my wife, Jennifer Dominguez, an excellent writer, and editor, and a true friend. My children Anna, Elijah, Olivia, Ivy, and my faithful yellow labs quickly fall in line after them.

I owe a special thank you to Jen Underwood. Without your editorial prowess, this book would have been twice as long, unreadable, and unfinished. It was a joy to create with you.

Chris Browne, thank you for your friendship, vision, and expertise!

"When I think of all this, I fall to my knees and pray to the Father, the Creator of everything in heaven and on earth. I pray that from his glorious, unlimited resources he will empower you with inner strength through his Spirit. Then Christ will make his home in your hearts as you trust in him. Your roots will grow down into God's love and keep you strong. And may you have the power to understand, as all God's people should, how wide, how long, how high, and how deep his love is. May you experience the love of Christ, though it is too great to understand fully. Then you will be made complete with all the fullness of life and power that comes from God.

Now all glory to God, who is able, through his mighty power at work within us, to accomplish infinitely more than we might ask or think. Glory to him in the church and in Christ Jesus through all generations forever and ever! Amen."

Ephesians 3:14-21

I trust you will find the information on these pages helpful
On your journey.
As you peruse the bits of material dappled here and there,
It is essential to keep in mind
The daily decisions we make in life
Are based on our conclusions concerning the nature of Reality.

Everyone is trusting.
The only way we live,
Eat, sleep, move, communicate, eke out an existence
Is to make decisions based on whatever we consider
Trustworthy.

As long as humans have engaged in conversation
And shared ideas,
We have differed on the object of

Our trust,
Our faith,
Our belief,
Our confidence.

Most philosophers agree that Plato and Aristotle's works on The
True Nature of Reality
Are a foundation for all human interaction;

And although epic cultural shifts have ensued…
Races and religions have been defined…
Empires have risen and fallen…

Every individual continues to make every single decision
Based on whom and what he or she trusts
As true,
As real,

As worthy
of trust.

And you will know the truth, and the truth will set you free.

Jesus
John 8:32

Don't copy the behavior and customs of this world, but let God transform you into a new person by changing the way you think. Then you will learn to know God's will for you, which is good and pleasing and perfect.

The Apostle Paul
Romans 12:2 (NLT)

SECTION 1
THE STAGE

CHAPTER 1
LOVE AND HONOR

"The birth of Christ is the eucatastrophe of man's history. The resurrection is the eucatastrophe of the story of the incarnation. This story begins and ends in Joy! It has pre-eminently the 'inner consistency of reality.' There is no tale ever told that men would rather find as true, and none which so many skeptical men have accepted as true on its own merits."

J.R.R. Tolkien
"On Fairy Stories"
from Leaf and Tree

We all have to pick a story to help us make sense of our world. The story we choose to trust frames our day-to-day realities. Erwin McManus, an insightful pastor in California, says that in our competitive, media-packed, modern culture, "the best story shapes the culture." He goes on to say that often the Truth is lost in lousy storytelling and falsehood is spread through a well-told story. I think this has been true for humanity ever since the earliest story times around warm, intimate fires.

We all live a life of faith. And consequently, we all live our lives trusting in one story or another. Furthermore, as we trust these various stories, transmitted from generation to generation, creatively invented or adapted, unconsciously consumed or intentionally adopted, we often forget these tales are human attempts to explain the inexplicable and to comprehend the incomprehensible. More importantly, we often forget (or deny) that these stories are theories. They are our best attempts to get it right. We all want to know what is really going on in the universe, and our stories—our worldviews—are the distilled essence of our collective efforts to describe what is Really Real, what is Truly True, what is worthy of trust.

My approach to worldview and, thus, philosophy, is practical and straightforward. It builds off of and extends the ideas of the iconic works generated by Socrates, Plato, and Aristotle on the nature and consequences of our beliefs regarding Prime Reality. In essence, these brilliant minds helped us see that the spiritual (the immaterial) and the material are the two essential elements for the fabric of reality. From this foundation I propose there are four primary storylines available to humanity:

- Idealism trusts that only the spiritual/immaterial world is real.
- Materialism trusts only in the reality of the measurable realm of matter.
- Monism trusts in the unified existence of the spiritual and material realm as one gigantic entity.
- Theism trusts the reality of both the spiritual realm and the material realm but maintains an understanding of real unity and real distinction between the two.

In this book, we will study these four main options in conjunction with the ways they answer several of life's essential questions and how these four options point to the fullness of Christ in a life-giving Christ-centered Biblical worldview. Doing this will give us clarity about and awareness of our own views and those of others, and we will begin to see how our objects of trust have shaped our personal choices. This knowledge will empower us to make intelligent and informed decisions about the multitude of religions and "isms" available to each human and to engage in honest, honoring dialogue with those whose views are different from our own and how the truth found in all worldviews points us to the Truth found in Christ. As St. Augustine says, "nay, but let every good and true Christian understand that whatever truth may be found, it belongs to his Master."

As you read this book, study these ideas, and examine your own choices with new understanding, I hope that your personal story—your life—will be shaped and changed. Therefore, this book has the potential to impact your current story in a significant way that then changes the rest of your story. It is for this reason I have chosen to structure this book as a Shakespearean play. I want this book to feel like an unfolding drama for you on two levels: first, as if you are an active character in it, participating in the story; and second, as if you are an observer of it, able to see and understand your own role and grasp the overall story as well. I have chosen a Shakespeare structure because Shakespeare accomplished this dual interaction with his audience: he drew his viewers so deeply into vibrant, lifelike stories they felt they were in them. They pondered the stories' ideas long after the viewing and were left with indelible marks on their minds, hearts, and souls. This is my high hope for your interaction with the ideas in this book.

From beginning to end, the viewing or reading of a Shakespearean play is an active thinking and emotional process. Characters and ideas and conflicts are intentionally presented in ways that intensify the viewer's or reader's engagement with the overall story. I have organized the sections and chapters in this book to have a similar effect.

Before I give a brief overview of the five sections in this book, I need to make my position very clear. It is essential for all people to have freedom and dignity to choose their personal beliefs, and I want this book to create a safe and healthy forum for exploration and authentic self-discovery. I have no desire to create a weak, insufficient, or biased description of a particular worldview to sway your opinion or manipulate your decisions. Rather, I want you to have a greater sense of self-awareness and ownership not only for what you choose to believe but also for why you believe what you believe in the context of so many options.

However, it is also important to note that particularly the last half of this book is an open, unashamed invitation to my readers to learn more about my understanding of Jesus Christ as the fullness of reality. In my years of teaching philosophy to students at a Christian high school, I have shared the four main "isms"/worldviews again and again, and I have come back—again and again—to a quote by G.K. Chesterton. In his book Orthodoxy, he writes, "They have torn the soul of Christ into silly strips." As I teach my students that each worldview is but a portion of the Truth—though we trust in the one we hold to as if it were the whole—I am convinced that the fullness of Truth and reality are found only in the undivided person of Christ. The story I choose to believe as the True Story holds Christ's birth, incarnational life, sacrificial death, powerful resurrection, and bold commissioning as its centerpiece. This center provides the main plot for the entire story of human existence—an unfolding drama we are all in. I believe all great stories point towards this Greatest Story and invite us to awakened and intentional participation in it.

Therefore, the last sections of this book speak to those who want to learn more of what it means to be a Christ-follower or who are interested in what authentic Christ-followers believe. I understand this does not describe all readers. If you are not interested in trusting Christ at this moment on your journey, I hope this book enables you to see why other people do choose to trust Him. Either way, this book should clarify your understanding of the major worldviews available to humans and also offer a fresh perspective of the Grace and Truth found in the person of Jesus.

I grew up striving to be worthy of the call by St. Peter to "always be prepared to give an answer for the hope that [I] have..." (1 Peter 3:15 NLT). I worked hard to be prepared to defend my trust in Jesus. Unfortunately, I was not actually living out the call as Peter originally wrote it. I was working to gain approval from man, which I was convinced would elevate my value as a human being. I worked from a self-satisfying desire to be recognized and loved; I cared more about my public image than I cared about the impact I had on the people around me. I learned painfully late in my journey that the verse actually reads, "always be prepared to give an answer for the hope that [I] have, but do this with gentleness and respect" (1 Peter 3:15 NLT). St. Paul compels us to do everything with Love or our efforts will amount "to nothing." Without authentic love for others, my words and actions are merely a "resounding gong or clanging cymbal" (1 Corinthians 13 NLT).

How does this truth apply to our study of worldview? Choosing a particular belief system, any belief system, without incorporating love, gentleness, respect, and honor will do you and the world a disservice. On this journey, it is essential to treat all people with dignity and respect. Much of Christianity has a sour reputation for being abusive in this global worldview discussion; unfortunately, we are known for trying to be "right" at any cost, instead of being known for showing love at any cost. I used to be part of the problem; now I am trying to be part of the solution. St. Paul knows what that feels like and two thousand years ago, he set the standard for Christ followers from God's perspective: "... while knowledge makes us feel important, it is love that strengthens the church. Anyone who claims to know all the answers does not really know very much. But the person who loves God is the one whom God recognizes" (1 Corinthians 8:1-3). With those words in mind, the approach to examining worldview that is described in this text is based on a foundation of love, honor, and dignity and supports the use of grace and truth as we interact with one another.

CHAPTER 2
THE JOURNEY

"The Journey is the thing." Homer

Life is an adventure. Thus I have structured the sections of this text to unfold like a journey. In section 2, I discuss the common denominator of trust. No matter which worldview we follow, we are trusting something. Everything is based on trust. The only way we live is to make decisions based on what we consider trustworthy, though we differ on the object in which we place our confidence. We give authority to whom and what we trust, and it is essential for us to understand that every decision we make is based on our conclusions regarding the nature of reality.

In section 3, we look at the four main "isms"—or worldviews—in which humans place their trust and how each answers some of life's essential questions. Idealism, Materialism, Monism, and Theism each hold a portion of the Truth, and each provides its followers with answers that influence how they live. In this section, I am neither endeavoring to exalt any one of these above another nor am I setting them up only to knock them down. I want to discuss and explain each one with as unbiased a view as possible.

Regarding the subject matter presented in section 3, I deal with only four basic views in their purest forms for two main reasons. First, this text is intentionally not a text on comparative religion or a grocery list of "isms" (there are plenty of those); this text is concerned with how to use the specific lens of philosophy to think critically about what we trust and particularly why we trust what we trust. This same lens not only gives us a fresh look at what we believe, but it also empowers us to understand why others choose to believe what they believe. Second, addressing only four basic views makes it manageable for us to learn about the particulars of our trusted beliefs in the context of other beliefs. Many writers have found other excellent—though more complex—ways to study and teach world religions, world "isms," and comparative worldviews, and I have been inspired by several of these authors, including C.S. Lewis and James Sire. The more straightforward philosophical approach offered in this book is not antithetical to these curricula and texts; instead, this book should serve to enhance your access to the other approaches.

Section 4 puts the "strips" back together and examines Christ as the fullness of reality. The Truth from each of the four "isms" is put together, seamlessly, in Him. We often work so hard to make our one piece or strip of Prime Reality into the entirety. We stretch it to make it fit every question or issue or reality we encounter, but only in Christ do we find both complete Truth and Grace. And only in the Power of Paradox do we find the freedom and integrity to live in harmony with the life-giving tensions implicit within Prime Reality.

Section 5 examines practically embracing the tensions of the paradoxes of Christ, for paradox is the only way to make sense of what we encounter in the world. Belief in Christ as the Real Truth requires an acceptance of mystery and wonder. Trusting in not only a Christ-centered Biblical worldview, but trusting in the person of Christ requires embracing paradox and, paradoxically, finding resolution. It also requires embracing the Truth as a living, loving, relational being rather than a philosophical construct or religious system. C. S. Lewis, who called the Christian story the "True Myth," wrote of this in his essay, "The Myth Became Fact."

> "The myth became flesh. This is not a religion nor a philosophy; it's the summing up and actuality of them all. For this is the marriage of heaven and earth: Perfect Myth and Perfect Fact: claiming not only our love and obedience, but also our wonder and delight, addressed to the savage, the child, and the poet in each one of us no less than to the moralist, the scholar, and the philosopher."

Lewis used several metaphors to express the paradoxes of Christ; I do as well. Yet, as I mix and match metaphors, I assume an essential truth: the metaphors are not reality. No metaphor is or can be; words and word pictures may point us to truth but can never truly embody (in the literal sense of embodying) the Truth, the Fullness of Reality. Christ himself used many metaphors to reveal parts of his fullness. In John chapter fourteen, verse six, He said, "I am the (W)ay, the (T)ruth, and the (L)ife." He said this not to provide a definition or axiom, but to extend an invitation: to see and know Jesus as the One to be trusted, as the One who sets us free, as the One who gives real life. Metaphors, like philosophy itself, are tools. Like maps, they are a means to an end.

Volume 2 of this text examines how trust in the paradoxical person of Christ leads his followers into paradoxical living and the exciting journey of authentic discipleship. For example, followers of Christ should be concerned with the nitty-gritty of life—how they do every small thing—and yet they must also see their lives—and everyone else's—as part of a much larger story. This paradoxical kind of thinking is personal, but it is also communal. It is sharpened and honed in community with others as we aspire to live as authentic disciples of Jesus in the True Myth of the Gospel of the Kingdom.

Early in my own adventure, I learned about this personal and communal way of life through studying the writings and lives of G. K. Chesterton, C. S. Lewis, and J. R. R. Tolkien. The individual writings of these three authors encourage a cogent, intelligent, and reasonable approach to start or continue trusting Christ, but they did not come to these conclusions in isolation. Chesterton's influence on Lewis was indelible and eternal. Lewis and Tolkien heartily enjoyed sharing conversations about philosophy, worldview, and theology with each other, usually in a pub with a mug over a meal seasoned with deep laughter. They dubbed their inspirational group gatherings the "Inklings." These regular interactions impacted the unique journeys each of these men traveled in their pursuit of the Truth.

J.R.R. Tolkien's books, The Hobbit and The Lord of the Rings, were intentionally designed as powerful, mythical, metaphoric, fantasy stories to point us to our roles in the compelling, real-life, mythical, fantasy story of life. In his unflinching, unquenchable quest for the Truth, G. K. Chesterton devoured the information in thousands of books authored by others. Ultimately, a personal relationship with Jesus Christ was the best option he found. Chesterton, Lewis, and Tolkien remind us that the book of Acts in the Bible (which tells how Christ's story spread to many people after his death, resurrection, and ascension) does not say "the end" after its final chapter, suggesting that the story is not over. That story is still being written today as people continue to live and grow together in relationship with Jesus as His authentic disciples. The last sections of this text focuses on the value of both personal journey and conversation with others as inspired by the works and friendship of Lewis and Tolkien and the ways they authentically encouraged and inspired each other.

I ask you to remember a few things as you read this book. First, it is not a traditional book on philosophy or theology or apologetics. Professionals in those fields have provided excellent sources for digging deep into those topics. I am a husband, father, brother, son, friend, and fellow pilgrim who is offering a practical and useful way to organize the information, questions, and answers we are bombarded with on this adventure of life. In many respects, I am offering it to you because it works for me in my day-to-day endeavors to love and, as Ulysses says in Tennyson's poem, "drink life to the lees." This book will not be able to prove The Truth to you in the traditional sense of the word "prove." It is not intended to do so; it is designed as a mirror for discovering your own object of trust and a map for you to use as you continue your journey and quest for Truth.
Second, I did not write this book to make you or anyone more "religious." I hope to show you truths that can break down walls, open locked doors, expose lies or fears, and invite you into joy, freedom, and love. I invite you to go beyond metaphor, theology, religion, trust lists, and worldviews into a relationship with The living, loving Being. The apostle John wrote of him: "You shall know the [Reality] [T]ruth, and that shall make you free." My unashamed, unambiguous, and ultimate hope is that this book brings you closer to The Christ—who can and will powerfully transform your life.

*"I believe in Christianity as I believe that the sun has risen:
not only because I see it, but because by it I see everything else."
C.S. Lewis.*

Thomas Merton, New Seeds of Contemplation

"If a writer is so cautious that he never writes anything that cannot be criticized, he will never write anything that can be read. If you want to help other people you have got to make up your mind to write things that some men will condemn." (165)

"That which is oldest is most young and most new. There is nothing so ancient and so dead as human novelty. The 'latest' is always stillborn. It never even manages to arrive. What is really new is what was there all the time itself all the time; the really 'new' is that which, at every moment, springs freshly into new existence. This newness never repeats itself. Yet it is so old it goes back to the earliest beginning. It is the very beginning itself, which speaks to us." (168)

SECTION 2

FAITH ISLAND

CHAPTER 3

CREATED TO TRUST

Everyone trusts. The only way humans live, eat, sleep, move, communicate, and eke out an existence is to make decisions based on whatever we consider trustworthy. This has been the case all throughout history. Even through major cultural shifts, the defining and redefining of races and religions, and the rising and falling of empires, people have made decisions based on whom and/or what they trust as really real, as worthy of trust. But, also all throughout history, humans have differed on the object of this trust. They have not agreed on where to put their confidence. Both of these are still true today. We still operate out of trust, and we humans do not agree on whom and/or what is worthy of that trust.

We give authority to whom and what we trust.The more we trust something or someone, the more authority we give.

Consciously and subconsciously, whatever we give authority to or have given authority to in the past, directly and indirectly, influence our current thoughts and behavior. Ultimately, we each develop personal lists of what we deem to be worthy of our trust.

These personal trust lists become the primary influence for how we view and interact with the world.

Unfortunately, not everything to which we give authority is worthy of our trust. Furthermore, we often find ourselves in situations in which others assert their authority over us even though we do not trust them. This type of authority often uses fear, inflicts pain, devises external motivators, and exploits ignorance to influence behavior. My teenage nephew Owen pointed out to me that it usually takes great courage to address the issues of trust and trustworthiness, particularly when it involves changing what we put our trust in or finding freedom from unhealthy, unwanted situations of imposed authority.

This is a great place to start our story. I hope that this book leads you into a story of courage and freedom. Facing the truth about trust and authority and potentially changing the motivation or object of our trust could possibly be the most courageous thing any of us will ever do. For some of us, standing firm in what we trust to be the truth and what we have found to be genuinely trustworthy in the face of opposition will take similar courage. This is where the adventure begins and, ironically, ends: in Trust and Courage.

CHAPTER 4
FAITH & FAITH ISLAND

The last chapter introduced this idea: We all live by faith.

Trust is the norm; it is the only option we really have to figure out the Truth about our existence. Since absolutely nothing is 100% verifiable by anybody—not scientist, not guru—by necessity we all walk this Truth Journey by faith.

We all trust our eyes, brains, tools, equipment, theories, methods, predecessors and professors, scientists and doctors, parents, teachers, and preachers. Sometimes these prove to be unfaithful, and we lose trust and break faith and even break hearts.

However, the bits of information we deem trustworthy, we tend to call "knowledge." When we find something perpetually trustworthy, we use words like “fact,” “proof,” or “logical truth.”

Many people have long desired to have an end to faith. They hope a staunch devotion to logic and reason can replace the need for faiths and beliefs which, they say, do not have “proofs” to support them. G. K. Chesterton points out the fallacy of this idea in Orthodoxy. “It is idle to talk always of the alternative of reason and faith. Reason is itself a matter of faith. It is an act of faith to assert that our thoughts have any relation to reality at all.”

To put it bluntly: every worldview is based on faith, even the ones that deny faith completely. This is an accurate and freeing statement, but it is not always easy for us to accept. It is hard for us to leave behind our blind confidence in “proofs” and our ideas that we can know things with 100% certitude. Imagine an island where everything in life is overtly based on faith. Every day, in every moment, all the people on the island live in acute, awake awareness that they have a perpetually faith-filled, moment-by-moment existence.

Imagine you are on a ship that wrecks near this island. You have taken refuge on it and can observe its inhabitants carefully. The natives wake up and have to believe they are getting out of their beds and then believe the eggs they are eating are real. They must have faith that their parents are really their parents, the coffee is not poisoned, and their tools will work. They must believe the sun is actually warming them and night will come in a few hours. You observe that these people live by faith all day every day.

As you read and imagine this scenario, you might be confused or frustrated. You might be smirking because the point of the story has "clicked." Maybe you're thinking "That would be insane! How could anybody live?" or maybe you have caught on and are wondering "Isn't that how we all live every day?" In my coffee shop discussions, I often get a retort such as "No way. I don't have to believe I ate my eggs this morning; I just ate them." Like it or not, believe it or not, the truth is that you are living on Faith Island right now right where you are. To make my point in my classes, I hold up a miniature blue and green globe and title the entire earth "Faith Island."

In my classes, we discuss this until it clicks for everybody in the room. Often I will offer an A+ for the entire class if someone can give me just one thing they can prove and perfectly verify with one hundred percent certitude. Take a moment and try to think of something right now. The painful turning point for the deepest skeptics comes when we collectively land on the conclusion that we all are very literally trusting our fallible eyes, hands, ears, and ultimately our often malleable and fragile brains to make sense of the world. And admittedly, all of these perception tools have been inaccurate at some point and could be wrong at this very moment. At this point, not surprisingly, it is reasonably short work to comprehend that all of life, for all people, all the time, is interpreted through the lens of trust and faith. Movies like The Truman Show, Matrix, and Inception often enter my dialogues. From me to you to every doctor, mathematician, clergy, guru, imam and hardcore skeptic, everybody exists on Faith Island, because faith (trust) is the only option for us every day that we live on this whirling, blue-and-green ball.

This idea may be shocking to us, but keep in mind that a life based on trust is not a bad thing. Despite all the cynicism and brokenness in our world, much is worthy of our trust, and a healthy knowledge and understanding of whom and what we trust can give us an honest sense of security and confidence. I call this a personal Trust List, and we all use our "Trust Lists" to help us make the most of our grand existence and daily adventures both individually and collectively.

At this point, it can be fruitful to write down what is on your personal trust list. Who are the people you have given authority to in your life? Whose voices are you listening to? What beliefs or ideas govern your daily life? You may want to take the next step of examining and contemplating the natural and even supernatural consequences of whom and what you trust.

Once you have a list, ponder who or what is on your list that is trustworthy; who/what should be on the list that is not; and who/what is on the list that should be removed. Consider what you do and do not trust and why. Are you on anyone else's trust list? If so, why? If not, why? Find someone, it could be anybody, and have a frank discussion on what makes something and someone trustworthy, and discuss the pain and complexities of broken trust.

In my classes, I encourage my students that their "homework"—not just for the following day, but for the rest of their lives—is to develop a strong, healthy, dynamic, life-giving, personal trust list.

There is some space for you to write down who and what are on your current trust list. After you fill this out, I encourage you to take time to ponder the reflection questions. After you've thought these through, I suggest having a conversation with someone (preferably someone you trust) about these ideas.

MY CURRENT TRUST LIST

- I trust
- I trust
- I trust
- I trust
- I trust
- I trust
- I trust
- I trust
- I trust
- I trust
- I trust
- I trust
- I trust

REFLECTION QUESTIONS:

1. What makes someone or something trustworthy?

2. What is on your personal trust list? What do you tend to find trustworthy?

3. What should be on your trust list that is not?

4. Is there anything on your trust list that should be removed?

5. As you contemplate your trust list, why do you trust these things? On what basis are they worthy of your trust?

6. Do you think you are on anyone's trust list? Why or why not?

CHAPTER 5
TRUST LISTS: THE CONCEPT AND THE TOOL

Your worldview is your view both of the world and for the world. You may not live what you profess, but you live what you believe. It's inescapable. We are great at professing, but how we live is rooted in our beliefs. Our worldview is not just a mindset; it is a "will set." It's how we live our lives, how we choose our priorities, how we adopt preferences.

A person's worldview is determined by asking the ultimate questions about origin, meaning, morality, and destiny. The answers touch every molecule of the universe—including you. The questions are ultimate because there are answers. (World)
William E. Brown

We're moving now from personal trust lists to collective Trust Lists, and we will look specifically at the Trust Lists of idealism, materialism, monism, and theism. From a philosophical and even a theological perspective, the Trust Lists of these worldviews reveal the foundations of their perspectives on reality and their interactions with it. These worldview Trust Lists form our core beliefs by providing authentic answers to some of the biggest questions of life. These answers also provide the substance of our shared "isms," religions, and ways, and they are closely linked to our personal trust lists. Even when people are unaware of this connection, the daily, continuous decisions made by people can be traced not only to their personal trust lists but to one of or a combination of the worldview Trust Lists.

As we develop personal trust lists, we intentionally or unintentionally pull from these four Lists or from an amalgamation of them. Unfortunately, many people are unaware of this. They haven't identified their own trust lists nor have they recognized the consequences of trusting the answers on the four Lists to answer the big questions they have.

Additionally, we often do not realize how much we are influenced by the personal trust lists of those around us. Their actions, choices, and conversations are also based on what they, individually, have chosen to trust, so as we observe them and interact with them, our personal trusts lists are affected by theirs, just as theirs, too, are being influenced by those around them. As people form themselves into groups, their actions, choices, and conversations extend into the broader culture and shape cultural identity, and the influence continues. Many people are unaware of how profoundly they and others are swayed by the broader macro-cultures of which they are a part, and this lack of awareness leads to miscommunication, misunderstandings, friction, and tensions in our homes and in local and global communities like churches, schools, neighborhoods, cities, and even countries.

There are significant advantages in identifying our own personal trust lists and, on a larger scale, the lists of those with whom we share community. Furthermore, increased consciousness of where we place our trust develops both self-awareness and shared awareness. Consequently, the more we know about ourselves and others' trust lists, the more we can engage in healthy dialogue and shared understanding with others.

As an example of how our personal trust lists are shaped by those around us, I'm sharing a question my insightful daughter, Anna, asked when she was five years old. Our beloved yellow lab, Pup, had died, and Anna said, "Papa, where did Pup go?" Though she was asking specifically about our dog, she was also asking what will happen when she dies, when grandpa dies, when her papa dies. It was and is a universal question. Like Prince Hamlet we all must ponder "the undiscovered country, from whose bourn no traveler returns," and this forces us to deal with the potential options of what actually happens after we die. Interestingly, how we answer that question directly affects the ways we approach daily life. Therefore, Anna's question was an important one, and my answer was also significant since she trusts me and has given massive authority to my iterations. My answer would influence how she frames the weighty issues of life and death in her unfolding individual story and as a growing member of our immediate community. In many respects, this is what directly creates much of the dramatic tension in this unfolding global story we are all part of writing.

The issue at stake for the sake of this section is there are different answers to Anna's question that have very different consequences, and the Trust Lists of the four major worldviews enable us to navigate this critical scenario and others like it. For example, if I were to approach the situation as an idealist, I would tell Anna that

Pup's physical suffering is over, and the perfected components of Pup's spirit have been united with the ideal, one, eternal state of spiritual perfection that exists beyond the broken, lifeless, material body on the floor. Pup has ceased to exist, but glimpses and moments of the joy, love, and beauty we saw in Pup's snuggles, wags, licks, and walks will live on because they found their source in the spiritual, eternal ideals of goodness, truth, and beauty that exist beyond this finite, incomplete world filled with death, pain, and decay. As Anna continues to grow with that in mind, she might seek solidarity on her journey in connection with the stories and themes found in Buddhism, much of Hinduism, and other religions or "ways" that pull from idealism.

On the other hand, if I were to approach the situation as an authentic materialist, I would tell Anna that Pup lived her life as well as she could and it is now done because her broken body does not have the ability to continually conduct the electrical impulses needed for reacting to her environment. I would carefully explain that anything we call "alive" has this end. We were uniquely fortunate to be a part of Pup's existence as she was to be part of ours. Pup's well-lived life full of experiences of joy, love, and adventure is now done, and we will dispose of her body before it starts to decay, just like we recycle or dispose of a broken electronic toy that cannot be fixed. As Anna grows, she might look for support to navigate the nuances of life and death in atheistic, nihilistic, and existential authors such as Nietzsche, Sartre, Camus, Dawkins, and Hitchens.

Alternatively, I could play the opening scene of The Lion King™ for Anna and approach this hard but hopeful aspect of Pup's journey like a complete monist. I would mention to Anna that life and death are natural parts of existing in the universe as a part of it. Pup is simply participating in the grand unfolding of the process of growth and transformation all existence goes through. The energy of life flows in and out of all living things, and Pup is connected to this life force. Her body was born and grew and lived and recently started the process of transformation into another form of existence through decay and dissolution. It is the unfolding, exciting adventure of participating in existence and transformation—like a little larva growing into a caterpillar, then turning into a butterfly, but then nourishing a baby bird and on and on. Some call this the circle of life. It will happen to all of us and has been happening forever. If she trusts this to be true, Anna might look to Taoism and Theosophy or possibly identify with the perspectives in the New Age movement.

Finally, I could talk about how God is a powerful, creative being who brought animals and humans into being. I could tell her one of the many creation stories like the influential one about Adam and Eve and all the animals in a loving, perfect relationship with their Creator and with each other. This would give some context for then talking with Anna about how this creative God has power over life and death and eternal life for all of creation. I could help her understand I do not know precisely what has happened to "Pup" because none of us is God. Though God has revealed his nature to be loving, life-giving, and relational, God has not been overtly specific and concrete about what happens with animals when they die. Therefore, God has intentionally put us in a position to trust Him, as the powerful, loving Creator, with what will happen to Pup now that her body has suffered the consequences of being a part of this world and being a participant in the unfolding drama of our existence. I could talk to Anna about God's eternal Kingdom where no one dies. As she grows, Anna might gravitate towards the theistic religions, their leaders, and their texts to make sense of the complexities of life and death.

These are four very different answers with vastly different consequences and potentially polarizing outcomes. This situation highlights the critical truth that the big questions in life—which occur daily and naturally all around us and sometimes come from five-year-old children—force us to use what we trust to develop responses. This scenario shows how this moment could powerfully influence the direction Anna takes as she continues her journey of choosing what she believes. I know, of course, that my response might not have much influence at all, but the point is that it could.

When Anna was faced with Pup's death, she accessed the perspective of someone she trusted. She willingly gave me authority in her life to help her make sense of the lifeless body of her furry friend, and I used what I trusted to craft the best response for her at that moment. As a philosophy teacher, I had many options to pull from to help her shape her perspective of reality and develop her own trust list and personal understanding of the story of her life.

CHAPTER 6
SUICIDE OF THOUGHT

Let's review for a minute. Here are the big ideas of the last three scenes: first, everyone trusts, though we differ on who/what we trust; second, our daily lives are shaped by our personal trust lists; and third, our trust lists are greatly influenced by others' trust lists, including the Trust Lists of our community.

But what if someone says none of that is true? What if he or she claims there is no point to trusting; says there is no real reality or validity; what if this person calls you foolish for trying to figure anything out? This is what we will discuss in this chapter.

In 1908, the seemingly prophetic G. K. Chesterton wrote, "There is a thought that stops all thought, and that is the only thought that ought to be stopped." Chesterton is referring to a completely opposite way of life than that adopted by the fully thinking inhabitants of Faith Island. Chesterton aptly called this opposite way the "suicide of thought." The internal monologue of someone slipping into the vortex of the suicide of thought goes something like this: "Since everything is based on trust and I have no means to verify anything, I cannot be 100% certain of anything. Therefore, I should not even try to figure out this reality thing. And anybody who does try is idiotic–because he or she will never be able to be certain, nor can he or she convince me of the certitude of anything asserted by either of us. Beyond lack of certitude lies the abyss of everything being unverifiable..."

This is a classic agnostic thought process, and the thought process of anybody who would like to wallow in the melancholic, half-hearted depression of latent postmodernism. In the mid/late 1900s, the influential thinkers of postmodernism expressed skepticism about life and existence, particularly about the self-absorbed humanism and overconfidence of industrial modernity in the early part of the twentieth century. These thinkers freely questioned the validity of everything, including human thought itself. This inevitably led to questioning even the validity of human existence and forced a philosophical debate on the substance and nature of thought itself. It is easy to forget that the post-moderns were and are simply recapitulating the idea of Chesterton's "silly strips," the idea that we can deconstruct the nature and fabric of reality. The postmoderns remind us we all have scissors and seam rippers, and we have the ability to dissect our interpretations of reality far beyond strips, down to minute pieces of thoughts and truths that we cling to as real and trustworthy—and then we can disassemble those as well.

Postmodern philosophers assert that our understanding of reality has been pieced together like my son Elijah pieces together a village of Legos, and, also just as he does with his village of Legos, we can take apart the whole thing brick by brick and throw the pieces into a bucket. Then we have the ability to reconstruct an entirely new village with the same pieces. Interestingly, we easily forget that on some level we actually do live in an existential reality, a reality in which we have chosen to construct our personal view of the world from the individual thoughts we have chosen to put on our personal trust lists, from what we have chosen as trustworthy. This is what the entire concept of the Trust List is built upon. Existentialism and deconstructive postmodern thinking explain how we all create our own version of little-"r" reality.

I find it helpful, with this in mind, to pause and sincerely honor the deconstructionists and even thank them for clarifying this foundational truth. It is appropriate to give them a high five or fist bump. Then, after a long, quiet, awkward pause, quite frankly we need to get on with reconstruction and, more importantly, with living. In G.K Chesterton's chapter "The Suicide of Thought," he urges, "We have no more questions left to ask. We have looked for questions in the darkest corners and on the wildest peaks. We have found all the questions that can be found. It is time we gave up looking for questions and began looking for answers."

The positive, encouraging truth gleaned from postmodern and existential thinking is this: when a commanding voice calls you to renew your mind or change the way you think, it is not only possible, it is a viable option. John the Baptist's infamous iconic voice still echoes from the wilderness and bounces off the cliffs of history 2000 years after he shouted: "Repent!" (which literally means "change your mind") to an entire nation of people. This John spent his life calling people to change their minds, their worldviews, and their personal trust lists. If this change were not achievable, he would have been insane. But it is possible, and Postmodern thinking gives us a glimpse into why it is actually possible for people to truly change what they believe and the way they perceive reality. Why is it possible? Because we have a real choice. Furthermore, because there are at least these four basic perspectives on what is really real, these real choices have real, weighty consequences.

That being said, however, the suicide of thought can make the idea and process of building a trust list seem vain, arbitrary, and capricious. Postmodern thinking in the late 1900s began to blend with an exceedingly existential philosophy that encouraged humans to only focus on one's personal, unique, individual, and thus, irrefutable interpretation of reality. This has convinced many people to believe there is no Prime Reality (with a big "R") but only fabricated, individual, unverifiable, subjective versions of reality (little "r"). Whether intentionally or unintentionally, these existential, postmodern thinkers have spread a lie: since nothing is 100% trustworthy, it is therefore not worth trusting anything at all. When people are persuaded to believe there is no Prime Reality—in other words, no objective Truth—they unwittingly embrace this lie.

Fortunately and unfortunately, the fact is that part of this lie is actually true: nothing is 100% verifiable! People are often distracted from the vital difference between "verifiable" and "trustworthy," and, thus, the suicide of thought is a formidable black hole which still has great pulling force in our culture.

I know many loved ones who have slid into this terrifying, dark, lonely abyss. Some have done so willingly, some unwillingly. The crux of the chapter is this: if you or I believe we have found something absolutely trustworthy, in order to maintain any thoughtful dignity and integrity, we have to admit that our direct access to this so-called "absolutely trustworthy" bit of information is through that which is not 100% trustworthy (our eyes, our brain, our senses). Therefore, we are left with the formidable task of figuring out what is worth putting our trust in and then making the most of our delicate situation.

Richard Rohr comments on this task in his work Creating Christian Community.

> "Much of Western culture is saddled with the conviction that humans must rationally create and explain all meaning for themselves. But this task is impossible, and so the search for meaning inevitably collapses into nihilism. The seeker gives up, assuming, "Since I can't figure it out, everything must be absurd and meaningless. There is no meaning, except what I manufacture, what I decide to believe." No civilization or community can be founded on this individualistic worldview because it is simply a collection of competing egos fighting for their dominant story based on private individuals' experience, hurts, perception, and education. This is most of North America and Europe today."

Rohr accurately states that suicide of thought cannot support civilizations and communities. It can even destroy them, and it can also destroy individuals. The hard, dark truth is that suicide of thought often leads to the suicide of will, and, sometimes, body. Fortunately—and this is more fortunate than we often realize—the truth that our entire interpretation of Reality is based on trust equalizes the playing field for all of us. In every household and culture, we are indeed like the inhabitants of Faith Island, each one of us living entirely by faith. Because nobody has the corner on the market or the ability to perfectly substantiate his or her understanding of the Truth, we all have an opportunity to engage in healthy, open dialogue. This can foster a compassionate community marked by honor and dignity. But this is only possible if we are humble enough to be honest about our inability to completely and objectively verify our own trust lists when we are in conversation with those who are trying to change their trust lists or with those who are struggling to find something or someone who is trustworthy.

I have found that the only way out of the vortex of the suicide of thought is to actually make a real choice. In the first half of the chapter Chesterton wrote on this topic, he takes his reader into the suicide of thought. Fortunately, for the rest of the chapter, he helps the reader see how to get out of it. This is a complicated matter, philosophically speaking, as you will soon see. But here we go. If we make real choices, then we do actually trust something. The natural result of making a choice for something means something is trusted and other choices and things are excluded. For example, if someone chooses to be a vegetarian, he or she will naturally exclude meat from meals. If I decide to wear my running shoes, I exclude my sandals. If my friend as a theist chooses to trust in Allah and the Koran to explain his existence, then he naturally excludes the primary tenets of atheistic materialism. Choice is the essence and lifeblood of Trust.

If you and I walk out our doors, breathe, eat, talk, interact with humans, live a life (even a meager one), we have a trust list because we will be making choices. And when we are making choices, we are exerting trust in that which we are choosing. When we choose, we are excluding. In doing so, we place ourselves somewhere on the grid of these four philosophies with their trust lists. We set ourselves somewhere in their various stories. This is why it can be helpful to see life as a journey of discovery. And, yes, as we travel this journey, we may find something untrustworthy and need to make different choices based on our experiences.

This journey of discovery requires us to keep thinking; keep breathing; keep trusting; keep living; keep finding what is trustworthy. If we keep the fire lit under the kettle of our thinking, our awareness will boil our thoughts down to meet the Reality in which you and I find ourselves.

We can despair during this journey or make the most of it. Interestingly, one of my students insightfully pointed out we can also distract ourselves or be distracted from building a useful, functional personal trust list. My preference, of course, would be that you consider this journey as an adventure, but, whatever your response, at the very least don't lie to yourself through constructing a false sense of certitude in your facts, knowledge, or proofs. All of life is based on trust, and we are all on this island of faith together, trusting. We must remember this as we mindfully create knowledge and facts and proofs out of that which is trustworthy. We are always trusting these bits of information, but, ironically, here is where the suicide of thought mutates into generative hope.

When hope dies, it makes hearts sick. King Solomon says in the book of Proverbs: "Hope deferred makes the heart sick, but a dream fulfilled is a tree of life." (13:12 NLT) This proverb is not about not getting what we want; it is about ceasing to hope at all. So, here is a bit of life-giving hope in a potentially arid and dry chapter at the beginning of this unfolding drama.

The suicide of thought does not actually exist.

I am glad you kept reading. It is an ironic, paradoxical truth. If the suicide of thought kills our ability to think, positioning us to stop trusting anything, including our own thoughts, the only way we landed in this suicide of thought is by trusting the thought that our thoughts are not trustworthy.

If you are trusting your thought that your thoughts are not trustworthy, you are trusting something. You are trusting that thought. Therefore, it is not the suicide of thought anymore. If you can trust the thought that your thoughts are not trustworthy, then you can trust other thoughts. The key here is it is a matter of choice. We choose which thoughts to trust based on their effects on our minds, bodies, and souls. Which thoughts will you choose to trust on your journey?

This truth is the bedrock core of all existence. We trust thoughts. If you can make a real choice, then this is the time to start choosing which thoughts you are going to trust. This is the adventure of life; this is the marrow and the impetus and the traction of life.

This chapter ends with a double irony. If we as humans cannot make real choices, then we cannot go into the suicide of thought, and, ironically and terrifyingly, we cannot get out of it. It was necessary to explore these ideas in this chapter, and you may need to continue thinking about them. Without choice, there is no autonomy and no real self-direction. There is actually no real self; there is only an illusory perception of "self" in which there actually is no "self." There is simply what one might call awareness.

Truth be told, without free will, there is no chance for real love or authentic relationship, and these, I would claim, are the foundational tenets of meaning for human existence. C. S. Lewis, a man who pushed atheism to its intellectual limits and who plumbed the depths of Chesterton's teaching on human will, notes this tension and potential in Mere Christianity. He states,

> "It is probably the same in the universe. God created things which had free will. That means creatures which can go either wrong or right. Some people think they can imagine a creature which was free but had no possibility of going wrong; I cannot.

> If a thing is free to be good, it is also free to be bad. And free will is what has made evil possible. Why, then, did God give them free will? Because free will though, it makes evil possible, is also the only thing that makes possible any love or goodness or joy worth having. A world of automata—of creatures that worked like machines—would hardly be worth creating. The happiness which God designs for His higher creatures is the happiness of being freely, voluntarily united to Him and to each other in an ecstasy of love and delight compared with which the most rapturous love between a man and a woman on this earth is mere milk and water. And for that, they must be free."

Thus, choice and trust are the core of all meaningful existence. Without these key ingredients, there may be life, but as has been seen here and as it will be further developed later in this book, an understanding of life without choice and trust has potent consequences. Inversely, the awareness of choice and trust creates an avenue for self-autonomy and self-direction; it creates an understanding of and motivation for an empowered, engaged, and meaningful life.

CHAPTER 7
REALLY REAL

Foundations of Reality

As I mentioned earlier, my approach to worldview, and thus philosophy, is practical and straightforward. It builds off of and extends the iconic works on the nature and outcomes of our beliefs about Prime Reality generated by Socrates, Plato, and Aristotle. In essence, these brilliant minds helped us clearly see that the spiritual (the immaterial) and the material are the two primary ingredients for the fabric of reality. Most philosophers agree that Plato's and Aristotle's works on the nature of Prime Reality are a foundation for all human interaction concerning Reality.

Over thousands of years, humans have developed Trust Lists based on their perspectives of the spiritual world and the material world. As mentioned before, a logical grid built from these two entities results in four foundational Trust Lists: idealism, materialism, monism, and theism.

This is the tension of the big story we all find ourselves in medias res on this planet. Generally speaking, these four different storyline options help us make meaning out of our lives. The law of non-contradictions (which states that a thing cannot be true and not true at the same time) and the reality of personal experience create distinctions between these stories that seem insurmountable. As explained earlier, we all live by faith, and we saw that no one has the corner on the market when it comes to verifying the truth of his or her story and trust list with 100 percent certitude. Every story and trust list seem to be true, at least to someone, yet we know intuitively and logically that all of the trust lists cannot be independently true at the same time.

My approach is not merely another shallow, slippery attempt to advocate relativism or universalism. Even though there are four basic attempts to understand what is Really Real, and from these four basic trust lists (or worldviews), there are hundreds of religions and "isms," there is ultimately only one True Prime Reality—one real storyline that is the unfolding the true story of humanity. On this pedagogical journey, I am intermittently accused of creating "straw men" in my approach to religion. These often well-meaning, individuals are missing one of the essential components to this approach to worldview: I am taking a philosophical approach, not a comparative religion approach, to understanding our connections with Prime Reality. My goals are to reveal and connect the Truth found in all worldviews. I am not combatively dismantling all religions except my own. With devout philosophers and religious leaders, I have worked to build an honest, accurate representation of all four worldviews with dignity and honor. Although this approach to worldview is not focused on religion, it will set you up well for the next comparative religion class, book, or conversation that you encounter.

Every great epic adventure story is driven along by tension, and there is plenty of tension in this discussion. Thus, we have the main plot of our story.

The Tension of the Four Perspectives

We will call these four perspectives the main characters in this story. The setting is planet Earth, and the plot is the quest for Truth. Each character is vying for the victory of being the most credible, the most trustworthy, and the most accurate world view! Pure idealists trust that only the spiritual truly exists as ultimate, eternal, prime reality. Authentic materialists trust that reality consists exclusively of the measurable material world of the periodic table of elements, electricity, and waves. Complete monists (or pantheists) posit that both realms are real and exist as extensions of each other—although dual in nature, they are necessarily one entity with no real distinctions or real separation. Sincere religious theists believe both domains exist, but the spiritual realm and the material realm co-exist independently, interdependently, and intra-dependently, with deep connectivity yet real distinctions.

These four perspectives contain and generate all the isms, religions, ways, beliefs, cults, heresies, ideologies, and worldviews that have ever been, and all seekers of Truth everywhere believe in some variation of one of these perspectives. Therefore, every individual will, by necessity, find himself or herself somewhere on the grid of these four Trust Lists when answering life's essential queries and tensions. The thrust of this entire opening section is this point: our interpretation of reality and, in consequence, the quality of our lives are based on what we trust. Therefore, the question of trustworthiness—of what makes something or someone worthy of trust—is a great question. It might be the greatest question.

This question of trustworthiness can shift the paradigm of the global conversation on philosophy, theology, and worldview. If we acknowledge that our different beliefs share the same bedrock of trust, we can change the tone, nature, and direction of our discourses from diametrical opposition to dialectical conversation. We must work together to pursue that which is ultimately worthy of all our trust, and we must be honest with each other in the process. We must not settle for any supposed "truth" that is not holistic, complete, loving, whole, unifying, and life-giving for people of all races, of both genders, of all ages, of all economic and societal "levels." We must, together, pursue a capital-T Truth that is worthy of being called Prime Reality, that unifies us, that is not simply one truth at the expense of all other truths, but which can hold many differences together. This capital-T Truth cannot merely be true here or there but must be true everywhere. If it is going to be called a worldview, it must be a view of the entire world for the entire world, for all times, not just this one, not merely my personal view of the world.

We can then say that the trustworthy thing or person that most closely aligns with all these ideas of Truth is Prime Reality, is the True Story of the universe. This is the standard by which we measure our personal trust lists and the Trust Lists of the four perspectives. For thousands of years, humans have claimed their personal and collective trust lists to be the Truth—to be Prime Reality. You probably have the same idea about your individual trust list, as does the group to which you belong. In this book, I am challenging you to not only examine the Trust Lists of other worldviews but to examine yours as well, to measure it by the standards of Prime Reality.

In the next sections of this book, I share the viewpoints of the four perspectives toward some of life's most important themes and the answers the four views give to seven major life questions. I created these Trust Lists to provide you with a clear map for approaching and understanding the daunting array of worldviews and religions and also to help you understand and evaluate where you, and others, fall on this map. Remember, in our search for peace and authenticity, we are all trusting one of (or perhaps a blended form of a few) of the four answers. Again, a key to unlocking the potential of this approach is to keep in mind that I am not explaining the nuances and minutia of all the religions and "isms." This book is not designed to give you the "what" or the "how' of religions; it is specifically designed to offer you a glimpse at the "why" of all of the religions and isms. When applied correctly, this approach will greatly enhance your understanding not only of why followers of other religions or "isms" do what they do, it will also help you know more of why you behave and think the way you do.

The lines between these four worldviews can get blurry as people seek to develop a personal trust list to navigate daily life. To help bring those lines into focus, I have added the distinctive adjectives: pure, authentic, complete, religious, in front the titles of the four views: Idealism, Materialism, Monism, Theism. These adjectives remind us that we rarely find people wholeheartedly adhering to only one of the four philosophical options. However, failure to find yourself drawing from these four lists usually indicates a lack of awareness of the object of your trust or of the natural consequences your choices create. Being unaware often results in feeling overwhelmed, underwhelmed, unfulfilled, unfruitful, or angry, bitter, and resentful.

Generally, appropriate alignment and awareness of the real consequences of our choices, especially those concerning the nature of Reality, create unity, peace, and freedom while simultaneously reducing internal conflict and confusion. However, the opposite may, in fact, be true: an awareness of the "why" behind what you believe could be quite painful and unnerving; nevertheless that pain is often the most effective path towards freedom and healing. Consider this as the difference between treating symptoms of sickness versus treating the cause and core problem of the sickness. An honest assessment of the object of trust and the outcomes of this trust ultimately leads to clarity and a more profound sense of ownership and vitality. Thus, this accessible approach to worldviews can be empowering, engaging, freeing, and inspiring.

SECTION 3
THE FOUR VIEWS

CHAPTER 8
PHILOSOPHY

"Philosophy molds and constructs the soul,
it orders our life, guides our conduct,
shows us what we should do and what we should leave undone.
It sits at the helm and directs our course as we waiver amid uncertainties.
Without it, no one can live fearlessly or in peace of mind.
Countless things that happen every hour call for advice
and such advice is to be sought in philosophy."
Seneca, Letter 16: On Philosophy The Guide of Life

Philosophy as a Tool

In the last section, we exposed the perils of not really examining our own beliefs, not knowing our own trust lists, and we also juxtaposed the optimism and hope that come from a clear, authentic, life-giving trust list with the dangers of the suicide of thought. Now it is time to move forward and continue or begin the process of discovery and examination. This is a wonderful process, with rich results. When we find what we believe is worth trusting—is trustworthy—and then we surrender to trust, we do not have to live either thoughtlessly or in the suicide of thought nor do we have to live in ignorance of what others choose to believe and why they have potentially made those choices. A healthy trust list has great power; it can lead to a thoughtful, well-lived life and meaningful, healthy relationships with others.

G.K. Chesterton pursued just such a life. He thought through his Trust List; he journeyed through life aware of his philosophy; he knew the "why" behind his beliefs, and he understood and accepted the reality of trust. Author Phillip Yancey, who wrote an introduction to Chesterton's Orthodoxy, dubbed him the "prophet of mirth" due to his ability to artfully engage others in sincere dialogue through wit, whimsy, and laughter. Because he knew and practiced all this, he was able to have enormous gratitude for his life. This is revealed in his poem below.

"Here dies another day
During which I have had eyes, ears, hands
And the great world around me;
And with tomorrow begins another.
Why am I allowed two?"

Chesterton had a sense of joy-filled privilege for his day-to-day life, and he believed life is beautiful and purposeful. This is what I want for you; it is the unfolding plot of this text, but I understand not all of my readers feel the same as Chesterton. It's not always easy to see life as a privilege because it is often difficult to make sense of the world and the daily decisions we have to make. So how do we do this? How do we discover gratitude for life? How do we make sense of it?

We use the tool of practical philosophy. Practical—or applied—philosophy helps us see that we already have a framework in place that guides our decisions and helps us "make sense" of the world. Practical philosophy helps us honestly examine and understand this framework—our views—and better understand the opinions of others. Therefore, it allows us to engage in respectful dialogue and relationship with others, even those with very different views.

Practical philosophy is an essential tool with vast amounts of power, so, as with all powerful tools, some instruction and caution are needed before we actually begin using it. Sometime during the first week of my classes, I hold up my grandfather's antique, leather-handled hammer. A hammer is meant to be used. It is not an object to be put on display or talked about or waved in the air. My Grandpa Sam, who loved to build, used his hammer. My tinkering son Eli, who loves to create, uses (almost daily) his hammer. Philosophy is a tool like a hammer. If we are not using it to build and construct our trust lists and worldviews, it is as if we have bought a hammer merely to carry it around and wave it. It will look, feel, and be ostentatious.

So philosophy, like a hammer, is meant for use. Here's another similarity. Though a hammer is a powerful, focused tool, almost anybody can learn to use one. My seven-year-old twins love pounding nails and building birdhouses or fairy gardens with hammers. Elijah, Anna's twin brother, is like my grandfather; he loves to use tools with purpose. Grandpa Sam was a master craftsman, Elijah is what we might call "on his way to becoming a master." Another key application is that a hammer can be useful for demolition and deconstruction as well as for building. If I need to renew my mind and change my perspective, I can use philosophy as a hammer to carefully pull apart the nails and boards of what I previously trusted in, to create space for an addition or a new kitchen—a shift in perspective. I could also use philosophy like a sledgehammer and swing it around for an extreme makeover, creating space for a whole new house—a new way to see the world and thus a new way to live in the world. Whether it is used for "big" or "small" projects, it requires skill to use the tool of philosophy, and, with expertise, the instrument of philosophy can be creative or destructive.

Because philosophy is a tool, it has neutral moral value. Consider everyday items like a cell phone or a car. In and of themselves they are morally neutral—neither good nor evil. Therefore, as tools, their value, usefulness, and moral implications are determined by the intent and motivation of their users. A hammer can be used to build, renovate, or repair, but it can also be used to smash windows or even skulls. The tool of philosophy has sometimes been used in just this cruel way; thus, we must be hyper-vigilant to use it in safe, honoring, loving, generative, and creative ways. Furthermore, due to the authoritative nature of the tool of Philosophy, a lack of experience, awareness, character, and/or skill creates an implied danger—like the difference between giving my young son a traditional hammer and a pneumatic hammer (also known as a "nail gun").

When we are not careful in how we use philosophy, it not only damages those around us, it hurts us. When we use philosophy with pretense, we become foolish. When we use it with ill intent, we become cruel. There has been and is too much abuse and cruelty caused by misuse of philosophy, as well as by the misuse of theology, doctrine, and religion. When any of these tools are abused and misused, they become toxic and destructive; they spread fear and confusion; they poison everything.

But the opposite is also true: when philosophy is used well, it is a powerful instrument for good. It leads to good thought and to good action. Margaret Mead says, "Never doubt that a small group of thoughtful, committed citizens can change the world. Indeed, it is the only thing that ever has." Mahatma Gandhi pointedly said, "Be the change you want to see in the world." And Anne Frank declared, "How wonderful it is that nobody need wait a single moment before starting to improve the world." Improving your own perspective of the world is a great way to start improving the world itself.

We will use philosophy to improve our perspective of the world. First, we will use it to understand and examine the framework we already have in place—the framework that guides our decisions and helps us "make sense" of the world. We can think of this framework as a house, a house we live in every day, that shapes our lives—whether we realize it or not. The trust lists and their answers to life's big questions have framed our houses. One of the goals of this book is for you to see the shape of the house you are in and, using philosophy as a tool like a hammer, to either de-construct it or re-build it with a greater understanding of it.

The house that you live in would be what some people call your religious beliefs, like the Anglican approach to Christianity, or your "ism," like atheism or pantheism. The isms and religions give us the day-to-day framework and context for interacting with people and making daily decisions, particularly concerning morality and relationships. We have already established that trust is the foundation of the house; it's what the house is built on. Trust is the concrete and the beams, as well as the screws, the glue, the nails, and the brackets. Trust holds the house up and holds it together. We established the truth that all the foundations for all the different Trust Lists are made out of the same material: every house, no matter its "ism" or faith, is founded on trust. The stronger your trust and the more trustworthy your materials, the stronger your house foundation and support system will be.

This section moves from the foundation up to the lumber and framework, to the plumbing and electrical work that is hidden behind the walls and paint. As we look at the big questions and the ways the four primary Trust Lists answer them, we will see that natural and in many cases, spiritual consequences are attached to the various options, just as a home's style is determined by the decisions a homebuilder makes. By the end of this section, after we have examined all the different belief possibilities laid out, all the different answers of the four Trust Lists, you should feel as if you are in a home decor showroom displaying all the decorating and detail options.

CHAPTER 9

TRUST LISTS

"Conversation is the thing." Richard Saul Wurman
Creator and Chair of the Ted Conference 1984-2002

The Power of a Question

One of the best ways to improve our perspective on the world is through conversation, through sharing our big questions and answers with others and listening carefully to theirs. These conversations can change views—and therefore the world—but these conversations are rare. Usually, people with very different trust lists avoid conversation about life's biggest questions, and often, when they do attempt dialogue, they end up talking around each other, and the conversation is unproductive or even divisive. Authentic, transforming dialogue requires the participants to have some common understandings: they must be aware of their own trust lists, and they must also have awareness and acceptance of others' trust lists, even those radically different from their own.

These are the kinds of conversations I want us to have, and this is why we will be looking at how the four major perspectives answer life's biggest questions. We will look closely at their Trust Lists. I hope that this will help you gain clarity on your own trust list and gain new hope, joy, peace, introspection, and momentum as you understand who/what you are trusting. As you do this, you will understand more fully the truths of Faith Island: that we are all trusting something, and we trust in order to resolve the tensions we see in our world and in our personal lives. The consequences for trusting various options vary greatly, but the truth of Faith Island allows us to see the "why" behind the beliefs. These deep understandings give us insight into others and acceptance of others and will enable us to engage in meaningful, productive, honoring discourse. And these are the kinds of conversation that can change our perspectives—and the world.

Before we move forward, however, we must first go back, back to the foundations of reality we discussed earlier: that the material and the spiritual (the immaterial) are the two essential elements in the composition of reality. This is the view of Prime Reality generated by Socrates, Plato, and Aristotle. The four major perspectives ("ism"s) are distinct from each other because of each perspective's views on these two elements, and these views lead to very different conclusions about life. This is the foundational premise of my entire approach to worldview. Our interpretation of prime reality (what is really real) sets the tenor and tone for one's entire trust list. It all starts with what one perceives and trusts to be really real. All the answers to every worldview question naturally unfold from here, lending this approach to worldview memorable, manageable, and meaningful. Here, again, are the four different perspectives:

- Pure idealism, which looks at only the spiritual as really real
- Authentic materialism, which trusts in only the measurable material realm
- Complete monism, which accepts both the spiritual and the physical realms as fully real with complete unity and no authentic distinctions
- Religious theism, which believes in the reality of both the spiritual and the material realms as deeply connected but with real distinctions

Next, we must review why these four perspectives developed conclusions about the nature of reality. Each perspective is trying to answer the big questions that arise naturally from the details of everyday life, questions even young children all over the planet have already encountered. As they have dealt with the death of a beloved pet or simply as they've been told reasons to share toys or food, they've bumped up against the mysteries of the universe. They began asking, "Why, Papa?" and "Why, Mama?" soon after they began to babble, and they will continue to do so. We are naturally inquisitive as a species, and as we tread the terra firma, soar through the stratosphere, and spiral into space (even if only in our imagination), we wonder and ask questions, big questions.

In this book, we will deal with seven of the big questions. While there are many more we must wrestle with individually and in community, these seven reflect questions every human has asked is asking, or will one day need to ask in order to help them understand themselves and the people and the world surrounding them. The seven questions we deal with in this book—and all questions—are the natural response to what life throws at thoughtful, introspective, aware, autonomous beings.

The big questions we will deal with in this book are very similar to those James Sire posed in his influential book The Universe Next Door. Although Sire did not originate the idea of the "big questions of life," he and many other philosophers made them colloquial, as they should be, and I tip my hat to them. I have reworked seven of the "big questions" for the focused purposes of this book and the Trust Lists. These seven are meant to be representative, not encompassing. I'm sure we could come up with twenty big questions or boil them down to fewer than seven. That is not the point; the point is that by practicing with these seven, we get familiar with the process of digging beneath the surface and looking at the trust issues inherent in every big question.

Dr. Charles Bressler was one of the most inspiring literary criticism professors I have ever had. In college, he introduced me to the basic structure of the four worldviews and the big questions of philosophy. He trained his students to analyze and interpret literature written from each of the worldviews and also to read critically through the lens of the views. It was life transforming, and I owe him credit for planting the seeds of this trust tool. I also learned from him the value of a classroom and conversation space where we can ask and lean into any of life's hardest and most complex questions. That is what I foster in my classroom and conversations; it is what I hope for my readers as well. I hope this text can loosen the tongues of those who want to become more comfortable with openly talking about those questions we too often shy away from—the big, hard, life questions. We often shy away because we fear unsatisfying half-answers and we dislike the answers available; we often shy away because life's big questions, when faced straight on, remind us again that all the answers are based on trust. This unsettles us, and we don't like feeling unsettled.

But avoidance does us no good, so let us move forward with courage. Let us explore the big questions and the ways we humans have answered them through a closer look at the four major worldviews. Let us pry open the door to our own views and the very different views of others. In doing so, let's create the type of understanding that will lead to further dialogue and further growth—because what we trust about reality has magnificent importance in our day-to-day routines as well as in the overarching storylines of our lives.

Let's begin by looking at the questions themselves.

1. What is the nature of Reality? What is really Real?

I have found this is a great place to start all conversations concerning worldview. This is the root of all four options, and each view is distinct in the way it answers this question. Most of the questions that follow are, at their core, related to this one.

2. Who or what is God?

Everyone has to interact with this question. Most philosophers agree that our answers to this question shape our entire life and directly guide our responses to any other questions. A.W. Tozer famously quips that your answer to the question "Who is God" is the most important thing about you. I wholeheartedly agree for the religious and non-religious alike. Depending on what we trust to be true, God may be a concept, a vocabulary word, a theory, a person, a spiritual being, oneself, the unnamable and unknowable, the creator... "God" has meaning for almost everyone, even the most popular atheists, for they understand that even if they do not believe in God, they still have to directly interact with other people who do, and they still have to deal with the popular vocabulary word and concept that infuses our global conversation. In a single class of just 25 students I can have individuals who believe God to be cruel, distant, immanent, intrinsic, selfish, egocentric, loving, generous, manipulative, uncaring, personal, abstract, disengaged, relational, abusive, dead, a joke, a lover, a friend, a teacher, a guide, a hoax... The 25 students I have in just one of the five classes I teach each day can have 25 different perspectives of God and thus 25 different approaches to their relationship with this Being and concept and hence their relationship with themselves and with those sitting next to them. What do you believe about God?

3. Who is man? What is mankind? What is a human being? We all have asked or are asking, "Who am I?" and "What am I?"

These are foundational questions that have profound implications, particularly in relation to the other questions listed here. Are we individuals? Are we distinct? Are we free beings, or are we a connected part of something or someone else...or both? Do we have non-material "souls" or are we simply a "sack of chemicals"? Are we puppets or self-directed or not directed at all?

4. What is the basis of and standard for morality? How do I decide between right and wrong, and who or what is the basis for moral authority?

This question begs whether or not morality is even objectively real. If so, where did it come from and why do we have to obey a particular moral code? This is why authority is a critical part of this question. Does a moral code have any real authority over me, and if so, why? If an ethical moral code does exist, can I change it? Why would I submit to an ethical moral code that I did not make? What is the difference between ethical more codes and religious moral codes or social moral codes? Do I get to decide what is right or wrong or does someone else?

5. What happens to a human at death?

Death permeates our world. What is death? Is death something to be feared or embraced? Is death an end or the beginning of the new real adventure or the continuation of this eternally unfolding adventure, or the end of everyone's adventure? Does death offer hope or does death end hope? Is death simply a concept, or is it nothing more than a vocabulary word? Can I define death however I choose, or is it defined for me?

6. What is the meaning and purpose of human history? What is the essence of human interaction and relationships?

These questions are not always included in lists such as this one, but I kept them as part of this tool because we all have memories, individually and collectively (as part of a family, a community, a nation, a people, etc.), and these memories profoundly affect us. This question helps us understand and define meaning for each day in the context of countless memories and eras of human history. When we seek answers to this question regarding history, we are drawn further into the mystery of origin—another big question. Deep thought about this question also gives perspective on the concept of "story," a story with a beginning, middle, and possibly an end.

7. Why are we here? Where are we going? What is the purpose of human existence? To be or not to be? What is the purpose of living for tomorrow?

Whether we realize it or not, we all spend a lot of time thinking about our purpose. We are enjoying or pursuing or denying or dreading or even despairing over it. Questions about purpose are often the most personal and influential of all questions, and our answers not only set the tone and atmosphere for day-to-day living but also for our lives as a whole. Like a soundtrack for a musical or movie, our understanding of our purpose is always present, providing a backdrop for the action of our lives, creating and sustaining the mood.

Seven Questions, Four Perspectives

Now we're ready to explore how the four perspectives answer these big questions. In this section, I want to give each worldview equal space and respect. Though earlier in this book I shared my personal worldview—that Christ is the fullness of reality—, please understand it is not my intention to set up "straw men" in this section—nor in any part of the book. I do not want to present these worldviews—each of them held by many, many human beings—in a fallacious way that makes it easy for me to knock them down. In the past twenty years, I have had many students share with me that they are atheists, Buddhists, New Age, or Muslim, and I tell them that if they pay careful attention to this philosophical approach to worldview, they should gain deeper insight and awareness into why they believe what they say they believe as well as into the extensive natural consequences of their particular trust list. If they choose to continue in their beliefs, this philosophical approach will also help them develop authenticity in these beliefs and in the practice of them.

Most of my teaching career has been in private Christian education, and nearly every year a brave student or two has sidled up to me at the beginning of the semester and covertly told me they are an atheist or a Buddhist (or a follower of something other than Christianity) and that they are excited to publically and privately destroy yet another teacher who will try to manipulate or shame their beliefs. While this is supremely ironic for the Buddhist, I calmly assure these students it is not my desire to ever manipulate or bully them or anybody. If this was you, I would tell you that if you genuinely want to be an atheist, you should pay close attention to this section because I can help you be a real, authentic, well-informed atheist—or Buddhist or whatever. Needless to say, as you can imagine for me in my high school setting, I've gotten a few phone calls through the years—and I have even been called to the principal's office. My goal, though, is the goal of all loving philosophers, and most loving parents and most seasoned administrators, regardless of their personal religion or trust list; it is to use philosophy to create a safe, honest setting for informed consent for one's beliefs. I want to provide you, anybody, but particularly teenagers, with the necessary tools, information, and clarity to seriously study your personal trust list and take literal ownership of it.

This book, then, is the result of a 20-year journey of dialoguing with others about their worldviews. It is in many ways an intentional collaboration with people whose trust lists are very different than mine. I deeply desire that this book presents each of the four major worldviews with honesty and honor, with the utmost integrity and dignity. Please be assured that many thought leaders, religious leaders, philosophers, and pilgrims from all faiths and perspectives have tested the authenticity of these lists.

On the practical front, I also want to make these views accessible, so I've chosen to present the answers in two formats. First, we will organize the information by the questions. In the next few pages, the seven questions are listed, followed by a short version of the perspectives' answers to them. (You may be like me and would find it helpful to see this all on one page. There is a visual of this as a grid in the guidebook that supports this textbook.) This kind of overview will allow you to compare and contrast the answers easily. In the second format, each perspective gets its own chapter, and its answers are more fully developed. This allows us to take a closer look at each view in isolation of the others.

As you read both the overview and the closer looks, I suggest you imagine you have just entered a big party and are being introduced to various people. Some of these people you know well already. You're happy to see them and feel comfortable connecting with them. You have a lot of common ground, so conversation flows smoothly. Some of your new acquaintances, though, are people you've only heard about (perhaps I told you about them in the past few scenes). You've never actually met them, but you've pre-judged some of them (and their corresponding worldviews and trusts lists), and you have a predisposition either for or against them. I know enough about human nature to realize that some of us are going to enter this party carrying baggage of hatred, condemnation, egocentric thinking, and alienation; some will enter the party with the desire to classify and delineate people with language such as "heaven or hell," "saved or unsaved," "demon or saint." This baggage will cause us to disregard, avoid, or even shun some of the answers wandering about the room while simultaneously causing us to gravitate towards others with admiration, curiosity, love, friendship, empathy, and compassion.

We must drop all this baggage! It is crucial; actually, it is essential, to keep this setting—that of a large party, feast, or celebration—in mind as you read the following pages. To maintain a tone of discovery and love, it is also essential to recognize your predispositions for particular perspectives and against others. You don't want to be the one who crashes the celebration with hate, rudeness, judgment, or dishonor. You and I are guests in someone else's house. We do not have to agree with everyone at the party or with all of the views expressed on the following pages (If you did so, you would actually be confused and not only look foolish but also be considered a fool.) But we must remember we are all guests, gathered in the same room for a bit so we can get to know each other better in a safe, healthy way, through open dialogue and fruitful, meaningful conversation, through thoughtful questions and active, engaged listening.

IF GOD INVITED YOU TO A PARTY

If God
Invited you to a party and
said,

"Everyone in the ballroom tonight will
be my special
guest,"

How would you treat them when you arrived?
Indeed, indeed!

And Hafiz knows that there is no one in
this world who is not standing upon

His jeweled dance
floor.

Hafiz
From: Love Poems From God, p.158

Throughout this "party," try to get a sense of the overall tone and landscape of each worldview, each "person," and find points of commonality between yourself and each view. I encourage you to read with a pencil, pen, or highlighter and mark aspects that resonate with you or connect with what you believe to be true. When my students and friends do this, they often realize that what they thought they believed is vastly different than what is actually on their functional daily trust lists. Let's move now into the first format to provide compare and contrast for each view.

The 7 Essential Questions

1. What is the nature of Reality? What is really Real?

IDEALISM (Platonism)
A pure idealist trusts that only the spiritual is really real. Reality is a state of eternal spiritual perfection.

MATERIALISM (Atheism)
An authentic materialist trusts that only the material (the natural) is really real; there is no spiritual realm.

MONISM (Pantheism)
A complete monist trusts that the spiritual and the material are both really real, existing as one entity without any actual distinction. Reality presents itself as dual with distinctions in nature, yet all of existence is ultimately one, universal, interconnected unity.

THEISM (Monotheism)
A religious theist trusts that the spiritual and the material are both real, yet they are independent (self-reliant and separated from one another), interdependent (collaboratively and reciprocally reliant on each other), and paradoxically intradependent with each other (unified and reliant upon each other as a collective whole, like a body with integrated dependent parts).

2. Who or what is God?

IDEALISM (Platonism)
A pure idealist trusts that the impersonal, eternal, perfect spiritual ideal is what people often call "god." It is absolute, complete truth, beauty, and goodness.

MATERIALISM (Atheism)
An authentic materialist trusts there is no objective, powerful being outside of the material. God is a figment of man's creativity and imagination, a creative idea or concept.

MONISM (Pantheism)
A complete monist trusts everything is "god." Because there is no literal distinction between anything, there is no distinction between god and humans and the fabric of the universe. Everything and everybody in the universe is an integral, interconnected part of the unity of life called "god."

THEISM (Monotheism)
A religious theist trusts there is a distinct God who is the all-powerful creator, sustainer, and giver of all of life. God is personal and has personality.

3. Who is man? What is mankind? What is a human being? (Who am I? What am I?)

IDEALISM (Platonism)
A pure idealist trusts that humans exist as one of the infinite, incomplete, imperfect replicas or shadows of the real, eternal, ideal state of spiritual perfection.

MATERIALISM (Atheism)
An authentic materialist trusts that human beings are a fascinating, unique, and highly complex system of matter and electricity that is incredibly aware of self and others.

MONISM (Pantheism)
A complete monist trusts that a human is a unique, unrepeatable part and parcel of "god." Humanity is part of the body of the universe, and the entirety of reality referred to as "god."

THEISM (Monotheism)
A religious theist trusts that humans are a distinct, wonderful creation made in the image of God but not possessing the exact nature of God nor existing as merely an extension or only as a part of God.

4. What is the basis of and standard for morality? How do I decide between right and wrong, and who or what is the basis for moral authority?

IDEALISM (Platonism)
A pure idealist trusts that all morality is objective and based on the nature of the impersonal, perfect, spiritual ideal, which is absolute truth, perfect beauty, and complete goodness.

MATERIALISM (Atheism)
An authentic materialist trusts that all morality is ultimately subjective and based exclusively or collectively on self, majority, and power.

MONISM (Pantheism)
A complete monist trusts that morality is entirely subjective based solely on one's individual preference and as a part of the interconnected, universal reality called "god." Thus, morality is entirely relative, yet it appears dual in nature due to the complexity, polarities, and variety found in the universe.

THEISM (Monotheism)
A religious theist trusts that all ethical morality is objectively based on the personal, all-powerful nature of God, who is perfection and goodness. God (and, by extension, God's word) is the standard for and author of morality. Many sincere theists follow ritual moral codes pertaining to personal and collective religious beliefs, distinct from ethical moral codes.

5. What happens to a human at death?

IDEALISM (Platonism)
A pure idealist trusts that when a human dies, perfection is attained. The human "becomes" part of (or is "absorbed" or is "purified" into) a unified state of spiritual perfection, and/or ceases to exist as a shadow of perfection and as an imperfect "self."

MATERIALISM (Atheism)
An authentic materialist trusts that humans cease to be aware of one's existence at the point of death.

MONISM (Pantheism)
A complete monist trusts that when a human dies, he or she literally morphs into another part of existence and another component of the universal reality, which is god.

THEISM (Monotheism)
A religious theist trusts that when humans die, they either obtain and sustain individual perfection or "wholeness" and exist eternally in continual relationship with the perfect, personal God or they remain in an imperfect, incomplete state and necessarily exist separated from God who is perfect.

6. What is the meaning and purpose of human history? What is the essence of human interaction and relationships?

IDEALISM (Platonism)

A pure idealist trusts that history and human memory are records of humans striving to escape nonexistence and attain an ideal state of spiritual perfection.

MATERIALISM (Atheism)

According to James Sire in his book The Universe Next Door, an authentic materialist trusts that "history is a linear sequence of events and phenomena linked by cause and effect in a closed system" (such as natural selection). Human interaction is literally chemistry and pure cause and effect.

MONISM (Pantheism)

A complete monist trusts that history and human memory consist of the repository of the collective memories of our collective coexistence and consciousness as god.

THEISM (Monotheism)

Again, James Sire says it so well; a sincere theist trusts that history is a "linear, meaningful sequence of events leading to the fulfillment of God's purposes for man" in an open system (Universe). History is the true, epic, adventure story of God's interaction with mankind; it is the real story of life humans are participating in.

7. Why are we here? Where are we going? What is the purpose of human existence? To be or not to be? What is the purpose of living for tomorrow?

IDEALISM (Platonism)
A pure idealist trusts that humans exist only to achieve and sustain an ideal state of spiritual perfection.

MATERIALISM (Atheism)
An authentic materialist trusts that humans create their own individual and collective meaning for life.

MONISM (Pantheism)
A complete monist trusts that every human has the exciting opportunity to experience being various components of universal reality—of god—forever.

THEISM (Monotheism)
A sincere theist trusts that at least one reason humans exist is to enjoy and experience a meaningful relationship with God, the Creator, and Sustainer of Life.

CHAPTER 10
PURE IDEALISM

A few words of the Buddha
"Be a lamp unto yourself. Work out your liberation with diligence."

"The Buddhas do but tell the way. It is for you to swelter at the task."

"Life is suffering."

"A wise man, recognizing that the world is but an illusion, does not act as if it is real, so he escapes the suffering."

Pure Idealism: We are striving to exist as spiritual perfection, the Spiritual Ideal (as God or as part of God).

Pure idealists trust that only the spiritual is the eternal fabric of prime Reality. True idealists have a foundational understanding that the non-material, perfect ideal has a timeless, beautiful, true, and good weight and realness to it that supersedes any physical attempt to replicate and materialize this true idea.
It often helps to think of people adopting this worldview as "Idea - ists." In class I have students think of the idea of their favorite car or chair. We banter about whose idea is the best and why. Then we discuss whether or not the perfect car or chair exists on our planet. Unfortunately, no one can point to a perfected car or chair in the physical realm; we can all think of the idea of the perfect chair or car, and many of the car and chair companies (barring planned obsolescence) are striving to make the perfect car or chair… but alas, we have not done it yet. Try it right now as you are sitting reading this text or listening to it. Think of the perfect – ideal – chair or car. If you are in a chair or car, are you sitting in or riding in the ultimately perfect one right now? Does it have no flaws, nothing that can be improved, and nothing that will break or run down? It really sinks in when I mention that were humanity to literally rid the entire planet of every car and every chair, the idea

of the perfect car and chair would still remain. There is much more to the discussion, but I think it will suffice for our purposes to simply add one more point. The nail is firmly embedded for my students when I have them all close their eyes and think of the perfect Being (it can be a human being if they so desire). Take your eyes off the page or pause the audiobook and take a moment and try to do so after reading the next sentence. Contemplate on this being—the ideal being who is always true, perfectly kind, authentically loving, incredibly strong, flawlessly beautiful, with vibrant, perfect, uninterrupted health… Did you imagine yourself as you are right now?. After 15 years of doing this exercise with thousands of participants, youth and adults, from all over the world, no one—not one!—has ever said they have pictured themselves. If you did not picture yourself as currently perfect and flawless, welcome to idealism, you have an idea of the ideal, of perfection; you have admitted that you are not that ideal; thus you are now ready to start your journey towards becoming this ideal. That is your "homework" for the rest of your life.

This understanding leads idealists to a greater awareness that this weight or realness of the ideal is manifested in a spiritual reality and is merely represented (re-presented), often poorly, in the physical. For idealists, this understanding applies to the entire physical world, but particularly to humans. Humans are necessarily imperfect shadows or incomplete imitations of the Spiritual Ideal. Humans are literally trying to become one with ultimate reality, which is an enlightened state of spiritual perfection. Currently, humans are imperfect and exist on earth only as representations of incomplete images of perfection. In essence, humans exist as potential. A pure idealist would say humans have the opportunity to achieve eternal existence in a state of perfection in the Ideal Spiritual realm. An honest idealist would also say this is a difficult achievement.

To further illustrate this highly abstract concept, take a moment to make a shadow in front of yourself. As you look at the shadow, consider these questions: Is the shadow real? What is the substance of the shadow? What is the shadow made of? The shadow is totally dependent on whatever is causing it, and what is making the shadow is not reliant on the shadow at all. The shadow exists, if it exists, because of the substance creating it, not vice versa. Try picking up the shadow with your hands or something else. Once again, welcome to idealism! In regards to this demonstration, that which is creating the shadow represents the spiritual realm, and the shadow represents the material realm. If the shadow wants to exist forever, it must become the solid substance that is creating the shadow. Otherwise, the shadow will cease to exist when the light changes.

Similarly, look at a photo of yourself. Try to imagine what the picture might have to do, might have to go through to actually become you (a living being) and not just an imperfect, incomplete image of you. For a pure idealist, humans are personally responsible for making themselves into the Ideal, for becoming perfectly good, beautiful, and true, for becoming really real and not just an image of reality. In the spiritual state, individuals will exist fully and eternally as spiritual perfection. In so doing, they will eternally escape the fate of nonexistence as an incomplete, shadowy replica, trapped in the finite brokenness of the material realm.

I am continually amazed at how many Buddhists in my classes, after a week or so of studying Idealism, find me after a class or in the hall to say thank you for helping them finally understand their families and culture's beliefs and behaviors… They often will say, "I never knew why they did all these religious things; I see so clearly now what is behind their language, behavior, and beliefs. I have a deeper grasp of what is motivating them each day. It finally makes sense to me." Again, I am not bashing Buddhism, quite the contrary; I love much of Buddhism, and nearly all the Buddhists I have met are some of the kindest, most tender, loving, and generous people I know! I am here to help people, especially Buddhists, understand more of why Buddhists believe what they believe. This is the power of philosophy in the context of worldview.

Buddhism, Taoism, and much of Hinduism construct trust lists from the Idealist worldview. If you are not a follower of one of those isms, take a moment and imagine how this big perspective on the nature of reality would instruct your overall outlook on life as well as your day-to-day choices. In the next few pages, we will look at how idealism answers the seven big questions. You may also find it instructive to research the idealist religions further and have conversations with people who follow them.

"Thousands of candles can be lighted from a single candle, and the life of the candle will not be shortened. Happiness never decreases by being shared." Buddha

"You will not be punished for your anger, you will be punished by your anger." Buddha

"I reached in experience the nirvana which is unborn, unrivaled, secure from attachment, and unstained. This condition is indeed reached by me which is deep, difficult to see, difficult to understand, tranquil, excellent, beyond the reach of mere logic, subtle, and to be realized only by the wise." Buddha

Answering the Big Questions of Life: Another Look at the Philosophical Trust List of a Pure Idealist

1. What is the nature of Reality? What is really Real?

A pure idealist trusts that the spiritual only is really real and Reality is a state of eternal, spiritual perfection. The material realm is an imperfect, incomplete, shadowy replica of the Ideal. In other words, the material realm is a broken, twisted, and warped shadow of the Ideal, which is absolutely good, perfectly beautiful, and purely true.

2. Who or what is God?

A pure idealist trusts that the impersonal, eternal, perfect, one Ideal is what people call "god." It is absolute, complete truth, beauty, and goodness. God is a state of mind and a state of existence. God is the Ideal One that is perfect, absolutely and forever. God is the Ideal state of being that is the pursuit of humanity.

3. Who is man? What is mankind? What is a human being? (Who am I? What am I?)

A pure idealist trusts that humans are not perfect; they are one of the infinite, incomplete shadows of the real state of spiritual perfection; humans exist merely as potential to become one with the Ideal and to finally exist as the perfected Ideal in a state of eternal, spiritual perfection and completeness.

4. What is the basis of and standard for morality? How do I decide between right and wrong, and who or what is the basis for moral authority?

A pure idealist trusts that all morality is objectively based on the nature of the impersonal, perfect Spiritual Ideal, which is absolute truth, perfect beauty, and complete goodness. All thought and behavior are aimed at achieving and sustaining this state of existence.

5. What happens to a human at death?

A pure idealist trusts that when humans die, perfection is attained and unity/oneness with the Ideal is achieved. Humans realize their potential, let go of the imperfect representation of self, and become one with the state of spiritual perfection. They cease to exist as imperfect selves and shadowy, broken representations of perfection. They cease to exist materially on Earth. Individually, humans cease to exist at all. In essence, real life/true existence begins at death.

6. What is the meaning and purpose of human history? What is the essence of human interaction and relationships?

A pure idealist trusts that history and memory are a record of humans striving to escape nonexistence and attain an ideal state of spiritual perfection. Human interaction is summed up and actualized in striving to escape nonexistence, either alone or together.

7. Why are we here? Where are we going? What is the purpose of human existence? (To be or not to be? What is the purpose of living for tomorrow?)

A pure idealist trusts that humans exist only to achieve and sustain an ideal state of spiritual perfection, to escape painful non-existence, and to exist eternally through becoming absorbed into/unified with the Spiritual Ideal, which is absolutely, perfectly good, beautiful, and true.

"Hatred does not cease by hatred, but only by love.
This is the eternal rule."Buddha

CHAPTER 11
AUTHENTIC MATERIALISM

When I have fears that I may cease to be
Before my pen has glean'd my teeming brain,
Before high piled books, in charact'ry,
Hold like rich garners the full-ripen'd grain;
When I behold, upon the night's starr'd face,
Huge cloudy symbols of a high romance,
And think that I may never live to trace
Their shadows, with the magic hand of chance;
And when I feel, fair creature of an hour!
That I shall never look upon thee more,
Never have relish in the faery power
Of unreflecting love!—then on the shore
Of the wide world I stand alone, and think
Till Love and Fame to nothingness do sink.
John Keats

Authentic Materialism: We are our own individual gods; there is no objective God to become, to serve, submit to, or to dwell with. We simply are.

Authentic materialists trust that the composition of Prime Reality is only that which can be observed and measured materially. No real spirituality or spiritual realm exists. Humans are beautiful, complex systems of matter and electricity who are subjected to an intricate arrangement of pure cause and effect and who are awesomely aware of their immediate, unfolding presence in time and space. To wrap one's mind around the tenets of materialism, it is essential to imagine our world as one gigantic system of electrical impulses. Electrons give movement to formations of matter and, therefore, give the perception or definition of "life" to particular objects. It is like a toy with batteries. No batteries, no life.

To help grasp this think of the elemental differences between a computer and your body. For an authentic materialist, this ends up being merely a matter of perception and substance; it is quantitative, not qualitative in a measurable sense. If the computer runs out of electricity, we add more; if it breaks, we fix it; if we can't or don't want to fix it, we recycle the parts or toss it in the trash pile. An authentic materialist quickly recognizes (without shame or fear) that this is precisely the same with a human body. If I were to run out of electricity, I would need to get more. I tell my students to run and grab the automatic defibrillator if I pass out and stop moving due to a heart attack. Plug me into it with the patches, yell "clear," and press the button so they can pump some electricity through my body so it can potentially reboot and re-calibrate and possibly keep running. If not, try to fix me, and if that won't work and materialism is what is really going on in the universe, share any of my working parts with whoever wants them, and bury the rest of my body in the ground under a tree… From this basic understanding of zero spirituality and the foundational principle of there being no objective creator, the rest of materialism naturally falls into place. The other six questions answer themselves logically.

In materialism, the impression of perfection or of the Spiritual Ideal is an entirely subjective, relative concept. Consistent materialists believe that humans can do and be whatever they prefer, so long as they avoid negative natural consequences. Simultaneously and paradoxically, a consistent materialist acknowledges that this freedom is arbitrary and that it is ultimately a façade. Life is actually an unfolding, passive adventure of random, electronic, reactionary impulses.

This was beautifully illustrated to me when my twins and I watched a compelling nature show called Planet Earth produced by the BBC. The scene in this particular episode was a helicopter shot of millions of caribou roaming across the tundra. We were in awe of the spectacle of so much life walking in great unity (my mind drifted to a favorite line of poetry from the "Fall of Rome": "and altogether elsewhere—silently and very fast"). I was jerked out of my poetry daydream by a squeal. "No! Run, baby caribou, run…" My daughter Anna, snuggled deep into my left armpit, was shouting at the television. A short-legged baby caribou, through no particular fault of his own, had become separated from the herd and his momma and was being left behind. The tension escalated through the roof when out of the bottom corner of the screen a wolf appeared. "Wolf!" Eli, Anna's twin brother, cheered as he pulled himself from the embrace of my right arm. "Go wolf! Go wolf!" Eli started chanting at the screen on my right side. "Run baby caribou, Ruuuuuun!" screamed Anna from my left.

This is it, I thought, the essence of materialism. All of life wrapped up in a cause-and-effect, life-and-death struggle. No choices, no morality, no autonomy, just reactions and causes, and more reactions and causes, the unfolding of electrons and chemistry interacting. Who am I to impose morality or judgment on the baby caribou or the wolf? Both are merely doing what they do—as all of us are doing every day all over the planet. Cause and effect, chemical and electrical impulse, life and death struggle. Anna started weeping when we heard the little caribou squeal as the wolf attacked it (off screen, thank you, Planet Earth), and Eli jumped up and gave a mighty fist pump of victory and a deep, powerful "Yes, wolf!"

A pure materialist simply observes what is unfolding all around without objectivity or judgment, simply observes and becomes aware of the unfolding mystery of life.

Consistent and authentic materialists unabashedly and wholeheartedly embrace the idea that life is ultimately absurd and beautifully or grotesquely ridiculous. Therefore, genuine materialists assert that humans can attempt to create their own sense of adventure, purpose, and meaning. Humans live out their awareness in the most personally pleasurable ways available while seeking to achieve positive natural consequences and avoid negative natural consequences.

Below is a list of some religions, isms, and ways that construct trust lists from this worldview. With this information in mind, you can learn more about why people of these particular "religions" and isms make the choices they make concerning day-to-day living and lifestyles. You may find it instructive to research these further and have some conversations with people who have adopted these lifestyles.

- Atheism
- Humanism
- Materialistic Existentialism
- Phenomenology
- Nihilism

Answering the Big Questions of Life: Another Look at the Philosophical

Trust List of an Authentic Materialist

1. What is the nature of Reality? What is really Real?

An authentic materialist trusts that only the material (the natural) is really real; there is no spiritual realm. Matter and electricity have existed eternally in various forms and states without beginning or end. That which is observable and measurable is really real.

The spiritual realm can be a figment of the human imagination caused by chemical or electrical reactions in the human imagination; the so-called "spiritual" can represent all humans have yet to discover, measure and understand.

2. Who or what is God?

An authentic materialist trusts that the individual human is his or her own god; there is no external, creator God in the universe. When the general definition and attributes of god (meaning the God others believe in) are investigated, they are revealed as either unreal ideas or as amplified human characteristics.

There is no objective, powerful being outside of the material. God is a lovely or ugly lie, a figment of man's creativity and imagination, or a generative, creative idea or concept.

3. Who is man? What is mankind? What is a human being? (Who am I? What am I?)

An authentic materialist trusts that a human being is a fascinating, unique, and highly complex system of matter and electricity that is uniquely aware of self and others.

Mankind is currently the pinnacle of existence in an infinitely intricate system of cause and effect. Humanity is the amazing realization of the ongoing potential of matter and electricity.

4. What is the basis of and standard for morality? How do I decide between right and wrong, and who or what is the basis for moral authority?

An authentic materialist trusts that all morality is ultimately subjective and based on self, majority, and/or power. Morality is inherently absurd at the core. There is no genuinely objective standard for good and evil for humans, nor could there ever be. Therefore, all morality is necessarily relative, based on value and agreed on submission to (or rejection of) a constructed system of human authority, community, and power. Furthermore, a consistent materialist will acknowledge that the complete lack of free will means there must also be a lack of culpability, and this adds another layer of absurdity to the idea of morality.

5. What happens to a human at death?

An authentic materialist trusts that humans cease to be aware of their existence at the point of death. There is no eternal existence of a person's spiritual soul beyond the grave because there is no eternal spiritual soul dwelling in the human body. Real life ends at death.

6. What is the meaning and purpose of human history? What is the essence of human interaction and relationships?

An authentic materialist trusts that humans, individually or collectively, "create" their own meaning for existence.

History and memory are ultimately absurd with no objective, overarching meaning or purpose. "History is a linear sequence of events and phenomena linked by cause and effect in a closed system" (such as natural selection) (Sire).

All human interaction is chemistry and pure cause and effect.

7. Why are we here? Where are we going? What is the purpose of human existence? (To be or not to be? What is the purpose of living for tomorrow?)

An authentic materialist trusts that humans create their own meaning for life. At the core, life is intrinsically, objectively absurd, because no objective meaning or purpose does nor can exist.

Humans live for whatever brings pleasure or the hope of pleasure.

Humans hope for or strive to create beneficial changes in their circumstances to increase positive natural consequences and decrease negative natural consequences.

"The madman jumped into their midst and pierced them with his eyes. "Whither is God?" he cried; "I will tell you. We have killed him – you and I. All of us are his murderers... Do we hear nothing as yet of the noise of the gravediggers who are burying God? Do we smell nothing as yet of the divine decomposition? Gods, too,

decompose. God is dead. God remains dead. And we have killed him."

Nietzsche "The Madman" Translated by David Chase, used with permission.

CHAPTER 12
COMPLETE MONISM

Tenets of Theosophy for consideration:

"The universe is the manifestation of an eternal, boundless, and immutable absolute Reality, which is beyond the range of human thought. This absolute Reality is the root of our real Self. Matter and consciousness (or spirit) are the two polar aspects of the ultimate Reality, from whose interplay proceed innumerable universes, in an endless cycle of manifestation and dissolution."

"The entire system of the universe, visible and invisible, is the scene of a great scheme of evolution, in which life moves to ever more expressive form, more responsive awareness, and more unified consciousness. The human consciousness is, in essence, identical with the one Supreme Reality, which Ralph Waldo Emerson called the 'Oversoul.' This ultimate Reality is shared by each of our particular beings thus uniting us with one another."

"The gradual unfolding of this latent divine Reality within us takes place by the process of reincarnation, which is an aspect of the cyclic law seen everywhere in nature, by periods of activity alternating with periods of rest and assimilation."

"The human pilgrimage takes us from our source in the One through the experience of the many, back to union with the One Divine Reality, but in full awareness. Our goal is thus to complete the cosmic cycle of manifestation with full conscious realization of ourselves, no longer polarized between consciousness and matter or divided into self and other, but unified within and united with all other beings through our common Source. This realization is enlightenment."

Complete Monism: We are already part of god (the Universe). Embrace and enjoy this truth and stop striving to become what you already are.

Complete monists trust that both the measurable material and mysterious spiritual realms co-exist as one (vast) entity. Monists, often called pantheists, assert that all of Reality is one reality presenting itself as dual in nature. This duality, or apparent dualism, is represented in unlimited perspectives and polarities as experienced throughout the vast complexity and tensions of life. It can be helpful to think of this as "Mono-Ism." Mono means one; thus it ends up being "one-ism." After reading this text Marti MacCullough, a friend and philosophy mentor of mine, pointed out that, according to the guiding principles of the literal meaning of the term monism, idealism and materialism both fall into that definition and would be considered monistic. She reminded me that materialism believes that all of reality is one reality and this reality is only the material. Materialism, like monism, posits that the universe is one gigantic, interconnected whole, with the significant difference being that the entirety of the universe is comprised of the periodic table of elements. The same is true for idealism, except that the "one essence" is spiritual. Marti and I pondered the implications of this realization for quite some time. The most fruitful outcome of our pondering was the realization that the only worldview that can authentically allow for any real relationship is Theism, for though it asserts a connection between the spiritual and the material, it also provides for a real distinction between the two.

I asked Marti for a better term to use. Neither of us could think of one, mainly because the word monism helps people understand the axiomatic driving principle of this worldview: the two realities of the spiritual and material are believed to be literally one entity. Let me take a moment to compare and contrast Theism and Monism. For theists, this exercise usually creates the "aha" moment much needed at this point.

Most theists believe humans have a spirit. The Bible is crystal clear on this issue. For example, there are many psalms (particularly 42) in which David talks to his own spirit within him. Many theists also believe that God's spirit resides within humans as well. A passage from the Apostle Paul in his letter to the church at Corinth helps drive home this point. He refers to the human body as the temple of the Holy Spirit of God. Thus bible-believing Christians believe that God's unifying, undivided Holy Spirit indwells humans—while each human also maintains the dignity of an individual human spirit. One way to say this is that our body is a temple for each human spirit to inhabit and also the temple where God's Holy Spirit takes up residence. For Christians, it is like sharing an apartment with a roommate (a powerful one!).

This understanding is often helpful for both monists and theists alike—because the language overlaps so much. Theism believes each individual human body has a unique soul that makes me, me, and you, you. But, as Paul iterates, the Spirit of God can also indwell a person, manifesting itself in different gifts unique to each person but also working as a unifying and connecting presence among people. Therefore, there is a unique, paradoxical unity-distinction in Christian theism. I will explain this further later, but it is helpful to touch on it here because this helps theists understand monism's idea of the one, unifying spirit indwelling everything. Unlike theism, though, monism has no paradox, for, in monism, there are no individual spirits. Nothing separates humans from the one, unifying spirit in all humans; therefore, humans are not distinguished from each other.

I hope this helped the light bulb come on for you. If it's still a bit dim, here's another example. At home with my twins, Anna and Elijah, and their sister, little Olivia Rose, our conversation could go something like this: "Do you have a human Anna- spirit? Do you have a human Eli-spirit? Do you have a human Livi-spirit? Do I have a human Matthew-spirit?" After each question, they would all nod, and I would then say, "Yes—four different human spirits. Ok, then, do you have The Holy Spirit of God dwelling within you, Anna, Eli, and Livi?" They nod again. "Do I have the same God Spirit within me?" More nods. "Good, I agree. Yes, I do. Are there four different God Spirits in all of us?" They shake their heads now, and Anna says, "There is only One Spirit of God, but it's God's Spirit in all of us, uniting all of us." "Great," I say. "Now, if you want to understand people who trust in monism, take the individual unique human spirit out of each of our bodies and what is left?" Livi shouts, "God!" I respond with, "Exactly, Livi Rose—nice work!"

At this point Livi would undoubtedly get up and do her happy dance, hopping around the room, and the rest of us would laugh, and Eli would seal the deal. "So in monism, God's Spirit is in each of us; there is no individual human spirit; God's spirit is what is really living. So basically I am God. And so are you. And God is what is moving me and connecting all things… connecting everything. God's Spirit is what is making Livi hop around the room, because in her body that is what God does." Eli and I fist bump. I add, "And since there is only One Spirit of God in all of us, we are all connected. Actually, a helpful way to think of it is to think of the universe as God's body. And because God is so big, of course, his body would need to be as big as the universe. One big universe that is all connected, just like your body is connected, different parts but all connected as one body, and one big God Spirit giving it life." In class, I can see the "aha" moment on my student's faces—though I usually have to say it three or four times… (So don't feel bad if you have to re-read the last few paragraphs).

For a complete monist, all of life is connected. Humans are part of all existence, and all of that which exists is already the Ideal for life. Thus, humans are already perfect as various parts of the one entity that monists often refer to as god.

God literally is everything, and humans are part of the everything that exists. For all of Life:

Emotions = Spirit = God = Truth =

Life = Material = Perspective = Emotions.

Like a human body that has many apparent distinctions and parts yet maintains a complex unity and harmony, so is the universal reality and integration of monism.

Humans each embody unique perspectives of god (the everything).

Humans have unlimited potential and power as god or as a connected part of god.

Humans embrace their unique preferences and seek a balance of all perspectives and polarities so as to wake up, realize, and utilize their real identity and unity.

Humans (along with all creatures and all parts of reality) grow in awareness of all perspectives as they embody the simplicity and complexities of life as part of the one, gigantic self.

Humans learn how to see all of life and all of life's tensions and polarities—the dualities of life—as a valid and valuable part of humanity's collective unity, and coexistence with all that exists.

Below is a list of some religions, "isms," and ways that construct trust lists from this worldview.

- Pantheism
- New Age

- Much of Hinduism
- Spiritual existentialism
- Tribal religions that worship Nature
- Theosophy

"...The currents of the universal being circulate through me;
I am part or particle of God."
Emerson in Nature

Answering the Big Questions of Life:
Another Look at the Philosophical
Trust List of a Complete Monist

1. What is the nature of Reality? What is really Real?
A complete monist trusts that the spiritual and the material are both real, existing as one entity.
The spiritual realm and material realm both exist, but they are one and the same. What we call distinctions and separateness is simply illusory appearance; there is no authentic, actual separation or distinction.
Reality presents itself as dual in nature through polarity and perspectives. However, all of existence is ultimately one universal, interconnected unity unfolding in various forms.

2. Who or what is God?
A complete monist trusts that everything is god. Everything and everybody in the universe is an integral, interconnected part of the unity of life called god.
Existence and reality are what people often call god. The cosmos is filled with duality and polarity as manifested in all of life (birth and death, dark and light, hot and cold, creation and destruction, et cetera); thus god has a dual nature in essence and in being.

3. Who is man? What is mankind? What is a human being? (Who am I? What am I?)
A complete monist trusts that a human is a unique, unrepeatable part and parcel of god. Humanity is part of the body of the universe, and the entirety of reality appropriately referred to as god. The spiritual component to existence resides within, flows through, and permeates every human.

Man is not truly distinct and separate from god, but man exists as part of the material and spiritual reality of the cosmos, which, in essence, is part of the entire being of god.

4. What is the basis of and standard for morality? How do I decide between right and wrong, and who or what is the basis for moral authority?
A complete monist trusts that morality is entirely subjective, based solely on one's individual preference as a part of the interconnected, universal reality called god. Like god (as god is manifested in the universe), morality is dual in nature. That is to say, god and morality are positive and negative energy, creative and destructive forces, darkness and light, heat and cold, et cetera, ad infinitum.

5. What happens to a human at death?
A complete monist trusts that when a human dies, that person literally morphs into another part of existence and another component of reality, which is god. The shared, united soul shifts into another part of the cosmos with another unique perspective on living as god.

6. What is the meaning and purpose of human history? What is the essence of human interaction and relationships?
A complete monist trusts that history and memory consist of the repository of the collective memories of our collective coexistence as god. Humans are connected to history as part of the eternally unfolding story of the cosmos (which is god).

7. Why are we here? Where are we going? What is the purpose of human existence? (To be or not to be? What is the purpose of living for tomorrow?)
A complete monist trusts that every human has the exciting opportunity to continually experience being various components of universal reality—of god—forever. Each human is here to wake up to who he/she is as a unique part of god and reach full potential as a distinct part of the divine existence and unity of god.

CHAPTER 13
RELIGIOUS THEISM

So God created man in his own image, in the image of God he created him; male and female he created them. And God Blessed them..." Genesis 1:27 & 28a

"Verily We created man from a product of wet earth; then placed him as a drop (of seed) in a safe lodging; then We fashioned the drop into a clot, then We fashioned the clot into a little lump, then We fashioned the little lump into bones, then clothed the bones with flesh, and then produced it another creation. So blessed be Allah, the Best of Creators!" Quran Surah 23:12-14

"I am a red man. If the Great Spirit had desired me to be a white man he would have made me so in the first place. He put in your heart certain wishes and plans, in my heart he put other and different desires. Each man is good in His sight. It is not necessary for Eagles to be Crows. We are poor... but we are free." Sitting Bull, Hunkpapa Lakota Sioux

Religious Theism: We are unique, individual creations hoping to become perfect (or complete) so as to dwell with God, our Perfect Creator.

Sincere theists trust that both the spiritual and the material are components of Prime Reality. While they are interdependent with and dependent on one another, they are also mysteriously intra-dependent, or, in other words, dependent within each other. Humans are unique, individual creations in the image of a free, independent, personal, and all-powerful Creator commonly referred to as God.

Although humans are created in the image of the one, perfect God as individual, distinct creations of God, humans are independent beings from God and do not possess the exact nature of God. Humans are created to dwell freely with God and enjoy some form of a relationship with God and God's creation.

On earth, humans exist as imperfect, incomplete beings, essentially separated from God's perfect identity and standards. Therefore, in order for deficient humans to escape eternal separation from their perfect Creator and to dwell perpetually in relationship with their perfect Creator, individual perfection and fullness must be achieved or received and sustained.

Below is a list of some religions, "isms," and ways that construct trust lists from this worldview.

- Judaism
- Islam
- Christianity
- Tribal religions that worship a Creator

**Answering the Big Questions of Life:
Another Look at the Philosophical
Trust List of a Sincere Theist**

1. What is the Nature of Reality? What is really Real?

A sincere theist trusts that the spiritual and the material are both real, yet they are independent of and interdependent with each other. The spiritual realm and material realm are both independently real, yet they coexist and interact independently, interdependently, and intradependently within each other in various forms and degrees and in diverse ways.

2. Who or what is God?

A religious theist trusts there is a God who is the all-powerful Creator, the sustainer, and the giver of all of life. God is perfect and necessarily good in nature and being. God is personal having a personality. God has full authority. God is the standard for and author of morality.

3. Who is Man? What is Mankind? What is a human being?

A religious theist trusts that humans are a distinct yet dependent, wonderful creation made in the image of God; however, humans do not possess the exact nature of God nor do they exist as only an extension or merely a part of God.

4. What is the basis of and standard for morality? How do I decide between right and wrong, and who or what is the basis for moral authority?

A religious theist trusts that all ethical morality is objectively based on the personal, all-powerful nature of God, who is perfect and good. God is the standard for and author of morality, as are God's word and God's character. Though this does not necessarily have to, this may include ritual traditions or cultural norms that many would call ritual morality, which is uniquely distinct from ethical morality.

5. What happens to a human at death?
A religious theist trusts that when a human dies, one of two things will occur based on God's and the human's choices in this life. Either the person will obtain or will have received individual perfection and exist eternally in continual relationship with the perfect, personal God, or this person will remain in an imperfect, incomplete state and necessarily exist separated from God. When humans die, they either actualize their true self and exist (or continue to exist) with God or are eternally separated from perfection and wholeness. For most religious theists, real life is both now and later; reality, and thus some form of relationship with God, is available in this life and continues after death.

6. What is the meaning and purpose of human history? What is the essence of human interaction and relationships?
A religious theist trusts that history is a "linear, meaningful sequence of events leading to the fulfillment of God's purposes for man" in an open system (Sire). History is the true, epic, adventure story of God's interaction with mankind. It is the Real Story humans are in right now. Humans are independent and dependent, autonomous and gregarious, possessing will and identity as self in communion with others.

7. Why are we here? Where are we going? What is the purpose of human existence?
A religious theist trusts that at least one primary reason humans exist is to enjoy and experience some form of a meaningful relationship with the Creator and sustainer of life. Humans exist in order to expand, enjoy, and protect God's kingdom. They exist to bring joy and honor to God and self through genuine worship of God, through loving, healthy relationships with God and others, and through the authentic serving of God and others.

CHAPTER 14
FRIENDLY CONVERSATIONS

On the following pages of this chapter are the seven questions. In the spirit of healthy dialogue, take this book and these questions and go have a friendly conversation. Start the process of getting to know what other people trust. Conversation is the best way to do this, but you can also watch movies, read stories and novels, and view art that extends from or express different worldviews. All this will help you to become familiar with the language and behaviors others use to communicate their trust lists, and it will aid you in engaging in dialogue. I recommend you go through the seven questions with more than one person—for the purpose of practice, of course, but more importantly, for gaining insight into different perspectives.

You have already learned a great deal about trust and about the trust lists of the four major worldviews. As you move ahead in your journey of discovery by talking with others about their trust lists, what you need most is a posture of listening—the kind of listening that exhibits honor and kindness and respect. Please keep in mind the tone we set for this section: that of a party or celebration, not a courtroom! Ask sincere questions; listen carefully. If you want to take notes while they talk, ask the other person for permission to do so first. Don't argue or defend; just ask real questions, listen, and learn. Remember, always, that you are a guest in someone else's philosophical house.

ASK. LISTEN. HONOR. CONNECT. LEARN. LOVE

The Philosophical Trust List of: ___________________

1. What is the nature of Reality? What is really Real? Ask the person you are interviewing to talk about both the material and the spiritual realms.

2. Who or what is God?

3. Who is Man? What is Mankind? What is a human being? (Who am I? What am I?)

4. What is the basis of and standard for morality? How do you decide between right and wrong, and who or what is the basis for moral authority in your daily decisions?

5. What happens to a human at death? What do you trust will happen when you die?

6. What is the meaning and purpose of human history? What is the essence of human relationships?

7. Why are we here? Where are we going? (To be or not to be? What is the purpose of living for tomorrow?) Why do you believe you exist? And what do you exist for?

CHAPTER 15
MY LIST

Take some time to ponder your own answers to the seven questions, to think about your own trust list. The seven questions are listed on the next couple of pages for you to answer. Before you write down your thoughts, though, you may want to look back at this section, paying close attention to any parts you underlined or highlighted, any sentences or paragraphs that particularly impacted you. Many of my students find a second reading very valuable. Because they already have a familiarity with the ideas (and therefore will not be surprised by anything), they can approach a second reading with an intentionally open mind, with thoughtful introspection.

Another thing that might help some of you honestly and thoughtfully answer the big questions is to have someone interview you. Some of you may also want to carve out some solitude by going for a walk or finding a quiet place to sit and contemplate. Remember, the most critical part of answering these big questions is that you do so with integrity and honesty.

ASK. LISTEN. HONOR. CONNECT. LEARN. LOVE

Big Questions and Big Answers of Life for Me

1. What is the nature of Reality? What is really Real? Consider both the material and the spiritual realms.

2. Who or what is God?

3. Who is Man? What is Mankind? What is a human being? (Who am I? What am I?)

4. What is the basis of and standard for morality? How do I decide between right and wrong, and who or what is the basis for moral authority?

5. What happens to a human at death? What do I trust will happen when I die?

6. What is the meaning and purpose of human history? What is the essence of human relationships?

7. Why are we here? Why am I here? Where are we going? Where am I going with my life? (To be or not to be? What is the purpose of living for tomorrow?) What do I exist for?

SECTION 4
PARADOX & PERICHORESIS

CHAPTER 16
OPEN EYES

We are now in the 4th section of our journey, of your journey. Before we move forward, let us, like the chorus in Shakespeare's plays, review the action thus far. In section 2, we established that all our beliefs and systems are based on trust. They cannot be proven and verified with 100% certitude, so you and I, like everyone else, are living a life based on trust. In section 3, we looked at the four basic worldviews and how they answer some of the essential questions all humans ask. You identified your own position within these views and were encouraged to explore the opinions of others and get to know people with different viewpoints.

Now it is time to do some evaluation of the four worldviews. Before we embark on this, I want to warn you that this process will likely involve some pain and struggle. It is not easy to take the hammer of philosophy to the worldview you hold dear, to pull up its floors and open up its walls and do a close examination of it. But it is incredibly important to do this.

If you have not read Plato's allegory "The Cave" recently—or ever—I suggest you do, for he describes a process of examination and discovery much like the one we are on. Here, for our purposes, is a brief summary. The scene is that of people who have spent their entire lives chained, by feet and neck, inside a cave, facing a blank wall. Behind them is a great fire and beyond that is the exit from the cave leading to the outside world, to the sun, grass, trees... The chained people, however, have never seen either the fire or the outside world. All they have seen are reflections and shadows on the cave wall in front of them. They believe these are reality. Plato argues that if these people were unchained and turned around and moved progressively toward the actual firelight and then beyond that to the outside and sunshine, this journey would be difficult. Their eyes would be dazzled; their senses overwhelmed; they would argue it was all a dream. They would believe reality is the shadowy images reflected on the cave wall, and these new sights are mere fantasies. They would say Truth was what they had before. Andrea Lunsford, in The Presence of Others, states: "Plato said this movement from darkness to light is like the journey the soul must make from the prison of mere sensory impression (appearance or images) to the freedom of true reality, which exists only beyond the realm of the senses." (467).

Though I am not holding Plato's idea up as reality, I do believe his allegory accurately describes the journey we are taking in examining our own worldviews and the worldviews of others. The light of the fire—and then the sun—is dazzling; it hurts the eyes; we are tempted to retreat to the only "reality" known before, for it was safe and comfortable. If we settle for an unexamined "reality," though, we are trying to content ourselves with shadows cast by dim light, while the sun shines outside the cave. "Better," says Plato, "to be the poor servant of a poor master, and to endure anything, rather than … entertain these false notions and live in this miserable manner."

Lunsford goes on to say, "(I)n Plato's system, what we can see with our eyes is suspect, a mere shadow; only what we can see with our souls is 'real.' In making this argument, Plato raises issues as old as Western history: What is 'real,' and what is only apparently real? Which is more valuable, and why?"

In contrast to Plato's view of reality is the picture presented in 2 Kings chapter 6 in the Bible. The prophet Elisha and his servant are trapped in a city surrounded by an enemy army. The servant is terrified, but Elisha is calm. The servant doesn't understand how Elisha can be so peaceful: doesn't Elisha see the vast army camped around the city? What the servant doesn't realize is that he is only seeing partial reality. What he thinks is the whole truth, is not, and this puts him in great darkness, great despair and fear. Out of this fear the servant says his one line in the entire story: "Oh my master! What shall we do?" (I am sure that could be colorfully translated if someone wanted to take the risk!) Elisha explains to the servant there is a reality he (the servant) cannot see, and Elisha tells him, "Those who are with us are more than those who are with them." I'm sure there was an awkward pause here as the servant stared hard at the enemy army before turning back to Elisha with a very odd look. Elisha doesn't bother explaining; rather, he prays! And his prayer seems a little unusual for the circumstances! He doesn't pray, "O God, please send your army!" Or "O God, please rescue us in some creative and unique way!" No, Elisha prays for the servant's eyes to be opened. This probably prompted another strange look on the servant's face. He already has his eyes open! He can see the trouble—it's right there to see! We don't know if he actually said any of that to Elisha—he only got one line recorded in the story—but we can imagine it's what he is thinking.

But then God answers Elisha's prayer: he opens the servant's "already-open" eyes so that he, too, can see all of reality, not just part of it. The physical enemy army is still there; it is real, but what is also real are the spiritual horses and chariots of fire that surround the enemy! Plato argued that what is seen with the physical eyes is not actually real, but this scene in the Bible makes it clear that in the biblical view both the physical and the spiritual are real and true. When the servant can see both material and spiritual reality, his perspective changes. And so does his emotional state. Again, our perceptions of and beliefs in Prime Reality directly correspond to our daily experience within Prime Reality. In this particular instance, Elisha's perception and understanding of Reality spared him the trauma and fear his servant experienced.

John in the opening musings of his Gospel calls Jesus the true light who gives light to everyone, the true light who shines in the darkness and is not overcome by it. Jesus, paradoxically, both sheds light on reality and is himself the fullness of reality. John 1 also calls Jesus "life" and "glory" and says he is full of "grace and truth." It is my sincere belief that Jesus is the fullness of reality, but we have taken bits and pieces of this fullness and parceled it out, building entire worldviews on just one scrap. Perhaps the fullness is too dazzling, too overwhelming for us, and so our splitting apart this fullness is an attempt at controlling our perceptions of reality, is a way of feeling safe and comfortable. Chesterton says we have "torn the soul of Christ into silly strips," with each strip holding only a portion of the Truth. If we want to make any steps toward seeing the fullness of reality, we must examine this idea. This is what we will do in this section; we will examine the "strip" held by each worldview as well as the consequences of believing that this one strip is the Whole. And, following the loving example of Jesus, we will do this in grace; we will pursue both grace and truth—together.

CHAPTER 17
CONNECTING TRUTH

"There is a huge and heroic sanity of which moderns can only collect the fragments.
There is a giant of whom we see only the lopped arms and legs walking about.
They have torn the soul of Christ into silly strips, labeled egoism and altruism, and they are equally puzzled by His insane magnificence and His insane meekness.
They have parted His garments among them, and for His vesture they have cast lots; though the coat was without seam woven from the top throughout."

G.K Chesterton
Orthodoxy

Examination of worldviews often creates a combative atmosphere, as if those holding different worldviews are in battle. Since one of the keys of this book is honor and integrity, and therefore we conduct our conversations with "gentleness and respect," we want to carefully avoid an atmosphere of religious jousting. Remember that we want this to feel like a party—and none of us wants to ruin the party by being rude!

Furthermore, this is a philosophical approach to worldview, not a religious approach. In our attempt to be gracious in our pursuit of truth, we are going to extend the metaphor of Chesterton's silly strips and think of reality as a painting, specifically DaVinci's painting "The Last Supper," one of the most admired, most studied, most reproduced paintings in the world. Now, imagine something horrible: what if, before the world ever saw "The Last Supper" in its entirety, someone close to DaVinci got his hands on a hammer and a chisel and got to work on the wall where this magnificent painting was directly applied. This conniving, devious entrepreneur then cut it into four vertical sections, and then sent each part to a different art collector, giving them the idea their section was a complete painting on its own. This would be a terrible thing: first, that the masterful painting would be chopped up; and, second, that the pieces would be masqueraded as complete entities. Yes, each section would still display DaVinci's magnificent skill; each would have a portion of the table, which extends the entire length of the painting; and the colors in each section would still be varied and beautiful.

In this metaphor it is essential to maintain the idea that the four pieces of the painting are from the original; they are original themselves. Yet what is also incredibly clear in this metaphor is that each section, or strip, even the one including Christ, the focal character, is incomplete on its own, incapable of telling the entire story of the painting. Viewers would not even be aware there was more to the painting, but perhaps they might wonder about the rest of the room beyond what is included in their particular section; about who is being pointed to; about the rest of the person whose arm was included in their portion; about how long the table is. These questions and wonderings would cause viewers to make assumptions, and some of these assumptions would certainly be wrong, for though each section is part of the original, it is still only part, and any attempt to describe the entire painting based solely on one section of it would fail.

Yet this is what each worldview does. Each takes its one strip or section and creates a complete view of reality based only on that one piece. The one part of the truth is not enough, of course, to support an entire view of reality or a view of life, so each worldview adds to the strip to make up for what is lacking. The truth, therefore, is there, but much has been added to it.

I want to be clear here in saying that these sections or strips are individual from each other. They are not merely different expressions of one vague truth; no, they are distinct parts—segments, if you will—of the whole, with the whole being greater than the sum of the parts separated from each other. What we will attempt in this section is to identify the truth held by each worldview and then look at some of what has been artificially added to the section to try to complete the picture. We are, in essence, "collecting" truths and stripping away the additions. Eventually, with all the truths/strips in hand, we can begin to piece back together the full painting; we can reconnect the Truth; we can begin to see the unity of all Truth. I have at times been accused of vague or veiled pluralism in my efforts to treat all worldviews with dignity and honor; this is not true: I am not a pluralist. There is a huge difference between saying, "All worldviews contain parts that are true" and saying, "All worldviews are true." There is also a difference between saying, "All things are based on trust" and saying, "All things are trustworthy." It is similar to the difference between admitting that nothing is verifiable with 100 percent certitude and stating that something is reliable and trustworthy. There are subtle but massive differences in these comparisons. The law of non-contradictions and the law of natural consequences will not allow the four different worldviews (which are based on different approaches to reality) to end up in pluralism, because by nature they are not the same thing, nor are they wanting to say the same thing.

Much earlier in this book, I made my position clear: I view the undivided person of Christ as the fullness of reality, as the complete painting. He fills the whole, yet he makes room for each of us. When we see all of Christ, the full painting, we can make better sense of all of reality, and we can make better sense of ourselves. Indeed, it is far more significant than this. I made the statement above that the whole of the painting is greater than the sum of the parts. The fullness of reality is far too great for us to completely understand it or to piece it together like a puzzle or to add it up like a math equation. It is something we can only get glimpses of, but even these glimpses of the fullness of Christ allow us to become more and more the selves we are meant to be, in loving relationship with others and God, as we are also meant to be. My dear friend and gifted art history teacher, Nate Leman, has helped me develop this metaphor and even has adopted it as the final exam in his class. He has shown me how powerful and enlightening it is to uncover the truth that all great art has the capacity to do collectively what I have done with this one painting. I will say later that all great stories point to the True Great Story, he posits that all great art leads us to the True Great Artist and his Awesome Art.

This is, of course, the ultimate goal, but to get there, we must pay attention to each individual "strip." We must evaluate and question and ponder. Many of you have had a hunch, an inkling, that something was missing or fabricated, or clunky about your current world view, while simultaneously knowing you are not completely wrong either! The same is true for your friends and loved ones who have different views of the world than you. In the following pages, we will examine what truth each of the worldviews holds, and we will think about the elements that have been added to fill in the gaps. We will find parts of each view that are valuable and trustworthy: this is the original strip. We want to honor that strip, that core. Examination will help us determine what has been added, what needs to be "stripped" away.

"[We] ...do not need to believe that all the other religions are simply wrong all through. ...all these religions, even the [strangest] ones, contain at least some hint of the truth." Let us move forward in pursuit of those hints (or sections) of truth and, ultimately, the fullness of reality.

In Mere Christianity, C. S.

CHAPTER 18
THIS LITTLE LIGHT

This little light of mine
I'm gonna' let it shine
Don't let Satan blow it out
I'm gonna' let it shine.

Over the years, as I taught using the metaphor of the divided "Last Supper" painting, I recognized I couldn't use it to move beyond this point. The painting allows us to see the unity of Truth—it allows us to cultivate a desire to see the masterpiece all together, to long for the unity of all Truth—but we need a different metaphor or image to enable us to see the distinctions of the different parts of Truth—the "strips" held by the different worldviews and the consequences of this division of Truth. I talked with my good friend and colleague, Jack Burgess, about this. Jack is an influential visual artist who thinks deeply about truth and reality and philosophy, and I knew he would have some good ideas. Jack's one of those quiet superheroes not many people know about (and like most true superheroes, he likes it that way). After hearing his suggestion, I told Jack his chandelier metaphor was brilliant (pun intended).

This new metaphor takes us beyond the painting metaphor in another critical way: it highlights the necessity of working toward a complete worldview. A painting is essential to humanity in a much different way than light; without light, we stumble around in the dark; without light, we can't see paintings. For this reason, a chandelier helps us understand the consequences of only having part of the full Truth. Hanging only one strip of a painting on our wall might strike us as looking a little odd, but it wouldn't be a significant problem; it may not seriously affect us because we wouldn't even know it wasn't complete; we wouldn't know what we are missing. Chesterton admits that in some respects all art is limited, the artist cannot fit all of reality into one painting; in other words, all art is only a "silly strip" of the world. If only one light out of the four on the chandelier is turned on, however, we would recognize the lack of light. We would miss the other three. We would want them on so we could see more fully and more clearly. This metaphor has particular significance concerning the allegory of the cave. Think of how many of us have grown used to two or three light bulbs being out. Some of us have never had more than one working bulb our whole existence.

The chandelier image also helps us primarily recognize that each of the worldviews does have light, truth, dignity, and honor. My atheist friend has light, as do my Buddhist, Hindu, Muslim, Jewish, and Pantheist friends. With this approach to worldview, none of the perspectives is entirely in the dark, and we can see truth revealed (lit up) in each worldview.

If you are reading this and you say you have Jesus—whom I have already claimed to be the fullness of reality—please don't skip ahead; don't assume you don't need this part. Each one of us has areas of both light and darkness in our views and perspectives. Even if you have Jesus, you will still have areas of darkness or shadow in your opinions of him, in your perspectives on reality, yourself, and others. Your personal understanding of Christ is not as big and full as the real Christ, as the actual person of Christ, who encompasses all of reality. If I had read this paragraph 10 years ago, my own religiously-inflated ego would have resisted its assertions. I most likely would have found myself getting defensive, haughty or even combative with this author who asserts that I may not fully understand all there is to know about God. I am thankful my search for Truth and my continuing journey is bringing me to a much different place.

Jesus wants us to grow in our understanding of him, and he provides help for doing so. Plato told us we must leave the cave on our own volition and power, but this is nearly impossible for us because we are not capable of even seeing or recognizing the fact that we are in a cave; we are not capable of identifying our own areas of darkness, and we all have some blindness or blind spots. We are genuinely ignorant on some level, not knowing what we don't know, and this is the darkest kind of ignorance. In the fourth act of Shakespeare's Twelfth Night, Malvolio is locked in a dark room and is being questioned by the fool, Feste. Feste says to Malvolio, "There is no darkness but ignorance." Malvolio replies from the dark cell, "I say this house is as dark as ignorance, though ignorance is as dark as hell." Jesus himself says, "If the light within you is dark, how great is that darkness!" Jesus knows the greatness of our darkness, and he, the very light of the world, was willing to enter our cave of earth. He is willing to enter our cavernous hearts and minds and to shine into our own darkness. He reveals light to us and then gently leads us out of the cave to where we can see his full light. He does for us what we are not capable of doing for ourselves.

In the following chapters, we will examine each of the worldviews using the chandelier metaphor. We will look at what truth is lit up by each view and what truths are shadowed by the "turning off" of the other lights. As you read the following scenes, it may be helpful to pre-imagine at least some of the chandelier concepts and grasp a picture of this metaphor in your mind. Each of the four exterior lights represents a different worldview. When all four are lit, the center—who is Christ, "the Light of the World"—lights up as well. When only one of the four exterior lights is turned on, then all the other outer lights and the center light are dark.

I want you to imagine yourself standing under that chandelier in a large, beautiful room, a room filled with things or people you want to see—beautiful artwork or beloved family members and friends, the latest gadgets or books from around the world. Imagine only one light is on. You can see the portion of the room that is under that light—with all that this portion holds, but the areas under the unlit lights are shadowed and dim. Imagine the longing you would feel to see what is in the shadowy areas. You know what is in them is excellent, but you cannot experience what is in the shadows unless all the lights are turned on. May this longing propel you in your pursuit of Truth. Truth is real, and it can be trusted. The journey from the wall of the cave out into the light is often tricky, painful, and gradual; it takes time to adjust to brighter light and see what is revealed by it. But this journey is imperative—and it's worth it.

CHAPTER 19
IDEALISM

The light of idealism makes it clear there is a spiritual reality and spiritual perfection. Something objective outside of what we can see with our human, physical eyes does exist. This is great truth; idealism tells us that all the hints we have that there is a reality beyond the physical realm are indeed pointing to something. There is a spiritual reality that is as real as what we can see with our eyes, touch with our fingers, taste with our tongues, and hear with our ears. Idealism tells us we are incomplete as we are, and this answers the longings we have to be better, to be more, to be in right relationship with others, with all people. This helps us make sense of the pain and chaos of the world surrounding us, for idealism tells us a perfect spiritual world exists independent of the broken, hurting one we are currently experiencing. This is why so many people adhere to, are drawn to, or at least admire and respect so much of Buddhism. Idealism tells us we have these longings for more and for something better because in spiritual reality there is an absolute, an objective reality that determines what absolute truth and beauty and goodness are. Again, humans have a natural inclination to admire real beauty and truth and goodness; somewhere deep they know there is gradation, and there is differentiation, and there is even a real standard for these things. While we all have different tastes and perspectives, Idealism reveals the truth that beauty, goodness, and truth are not arbitrary, based solely on individual or even societal norms; they are absolute, based on and decided by the one absolute, objective reality: the one Perfect Ideal, God. Idealism, therefore, has given humanity a standard outside themselves, an absolute standard, a rock-solid, eternal, unchanging standard. In this standard, idealism has also provided all humans a goal: to be perfect and whole, to be like God, even to attempt union with God—to become one with the perfect, spiritual ideal. Much of Idealism in the religious sphere will also point humanity towards the insight that if there is any spiritual truth, goodness, and beauty within us, it is from the One Source of Goodness, Truth, and Beauty.

These are great truths, but Idealism has built an entire reality on these truths alone, and this leaves us with questions; it leaves us living with some deep shadows. For example, in Pure Idealism (as seen in devout Buddhism and some aspects of Hinduism) the Perfect Ideal can be vague and impersonal; it ends up being abstract and static. It can be detached and without personality. There is little or no relationship with this Ideal other than it being a conceptual goal to strive for, and idealism offers no personal and relational help from a perfect being in attaining this goal. The Perfect Spiritual Ideal tends to be much more a state of being (like "Nirvana") rather than a Being itself. Nirvana does not have eyes or ears or hands or a heart. The Oxford English Dictionary offers this definition for Nirvana: "a transcendent state in which there is neither suffering, desire, nor sense of self, and the subject is released from the effects of karma and the cycle of death and rebirth. It represents the final goal of Buddhism." Hinduism would assert much of this as well.

This has unfortunate consequences when it is followed all the way to its conclusion. If spiritually speaking, God is perfection, and the ultimate eternal standard is spiritual perfection, then consequently humans will find themselves endeavoring and striving not merely to be like god, or subserviently dwell alongside of God, or live with God in solidarity, but ultimately strive to become God. Hinduism, alongside Buddhism, pulls from this truth, noting that if there is any Goodness, Truth, and Beauty in a human, it is because "God (the One) is dwelling in me as me." This sounds like a powerful, beautiful perspective until we settle into the hollow understanding that if it is true, then there is no "me"! This is one of the main tenets of Buddhism and Hinduism: there is no self, no "me"; there is only God. Union with God is not like marriage, in which the two become one and yet paradoxically remain two; union with god is absorption into God, at the expense and detachment of self. One loses oneself in God—and thus ends up without a self. While that may sound great at first hearing, it means for pure idealists there is no "other" for God to Love, other than God, who is not a being, who does not even have a self. Thus there is no real Love because love at least requires "two"—and in Idealism, there is only "one." This point always reminds me of a three-hour lunch I had with a devout Buddhist who concluded I was selfish for wanting to have and maintain a "self."

Furthermore, honest humans know humans cannot become perfect on their own, but this is what Idealism sets in front of them: an endless striving after an impossible goal. In much of Idealist thought, each human, upon achieving perfection, is absorbed into the Ideal and ceases to be an individual self. This also means the material world has no lasting value and is not real; it does not matter; it is merely a shadow of spiritual reality and is expected to be shed and left behind more and more—and, ultimately, left behind entirely—as spiritual perfection is attained. This train of thought is what leads so many Buddhists to the wholesale rejection of the material realm as pure shadow and even evil. Though some embrace this concept of becoming one spiritually with the ideal "One," it assuredly undercuts a basic human desire to be unique, to be a person, to retain a sense of self and relationship with others beyond this material world. We all want to be the best version of ourselves, but, in almost all cases, we want to still be ourselves, and Idealism tells us we are not really real until we lose all sense of self and become one with the Ideal Spiritual One, which is a concept of "Self." Real life in Idealism starts after death, but it is a life without any sense of individuality. The Buddha pointedly states: "life is suffering" and this is a statement based upon the premise that life before death is an illusion, a shadow of life—is not life at all.

Idealism's lights are shining on a beautiful Ideal, but it is a sterile Ideal, separate and so far above us, we cannot touch it. This Ideal, though, reveals deep longings within us: first, that we have a desire and a need for an absolute, for a standard of goodness and beauty and truth that is separate from us but accessible to us, a standard not made by us, a standard that is not relative. Second, that we want to be like this ideal but still retain our identity, both our spiritual and material identity; and third, that we are incapable of making ourselves perfect. In class I have to repeat this sentence multiple times almost like a mantra: "If I need to make myself perfect, I would need to be perfect in order to do so perfectly; a perfect person is the only person who could perfectly make themselves perfect. I know I am not perfect, and therefore I would not be capable of making myself perfect perfectly." We need help, and deep down, beneath our pride and self-sufficiency, we want help.

C.S. Lewis mentions this concept in Mere Christianity in his chapter titled "The Perfect Penitent." He says,

> "Now what was the sort of 'hole' man had got himself into? He had tried to set up on his own, to behave as if he belonged to himself. In other words, fallen man is not simply an imperfect creature who needs improvement: he is a rebel who must lay down his arms. Laying down your arms, surrendering, saying you are sorry, realizing that you have been on the wrong track and getting ready to start life over again from the ground floor—that is the only way out of a 'hole.' This process of surrender—this movement full speed astern—is what Christians call repentance. Now repentance is no fun at all. It is something much harder than merely eating humble pie. It means unlearning all the self-conceit and self-will that we have been training ourselves into for thousands of years. It means killing part of yourself, undergoing a kind of death. In fact, it needs a good man to repent. And here comes the catch. Only a bad person needs to repent: only a good person can repent perfectly. The worse you are the more you need it and the less you can do it. The only person who could do it perfectly would be a perfect person—and he would not need it."

Find a friend or two and take a few moments, close your eyes, and practice thinking of perfect ideas, such as chairs, cars, cats, etc.; have fun debating the relative standards of perfection as you discuss whose ideals are the best. It is easy to come to the conclusion that nothing on earth is perfect or permanent. The bright light of idealism shines on us at this moment. Take it one step further to illustrate a fundamental principle in idealism. Re-enact the moment from earlier, but now with a group of people and clear your minds and keenly focus on the perfect being. Feel free to put this text down right now and do it. Have the group close all eyes and think of the ideal being: with no flaws, entirely true, perfectly beautiful, perfectly honest, perfectly moral, utterly powerful, filled with vigor and life, perfectly good, with a perfect history and legacy, entirely generous, perfectly loving.... Take some time to meditate and ponder on this being. Focus all your thoughts on this being. Wait until every person in the group has a being in mind, and then quietly ask if anybody in the room is focusing on themselves. I have never had anyone say yes—and mean it. This, in essence, is the piercing light of idealism; we are all, on some level, idealists at this point.

Keep in mind that in order to be that imagined perfect being, you would by necessity have to stop being yourself as you are right now—because you just admitted you are not that being; additionally, in Idealism there is only one perfect being—rather, one perfect state of being—and all others are subject to that one. Our goal in Idealism would be to figure out which one is the real one and then all strive to attain unity with that one." Even if you, or someone in your group, were to name "Jesus" as your perfect being—a great answer—I remind you that though you may have been taught to "be like Jesus," the Gospels do not tell us to let go of ourselves and "become Jesus." We are told in Scripture that Jesus wants a relationship with us, that Jesus is, in essence, our older brother in the family of God the Father. Jesus was fully, materially, and spiritually alive and himself when he lived as God in the flesh, filled with God's Holy Spirit. I, too, need to be fully me, with my own individual spirit, yet with God's Spirit also fully in me. I am to be filled with God's Holy Spirit, as Jesus was, but be fully me, not God. This is only possible with the spiritual and physical distinction revealed by the Light of Theism, with the spiritual Unity revealed by the Light of Monism, and with the physicality revealed by the hard, solid light of Materialism.

In turning off the light and the distinctions found in Theism, an Idealist turns off the opportunity for there to be a real autonomous "self" in loving relationship with a real and distinct "Creator" of that self. In turning off the physical light of Materialism, the Idealist turns off the bodily presence of real selves that matter here and now and are individual and infinitely unique. In turning off the unifying light of Monism, an Idealist has turned off what allows the spiritual and material to be united and connected in eternal, sustaining, life-giving unity.

In the third chapter of his famous letter to the church in Rome, the apostle Paul states in verse twenty-three: "for everyone has sinned; we all fall short of God's glorious standard." This is much of the essence of what is meant when an Idealist admits he or she is not perfect. Furthermore, what is this sentence essentially saying in the light of Idealism? In Idealism the onus for attaining perfect unity with the spiritual ideal lies in the shadowy image of that ideal. It is like a picture of a person trying to attain actual existence as that person. The picture hopes, through perpetual striving and hard work, to become one with the living person. This is an impossible task: for a lifeless, two- dimensional object to make itself three-dimensional and then give itself life. In Christ-centered Theism the Good News of the gospel is that God so loved us, His unique creation made in His image, that he chose to make those who have become imperfect, perfect—individually and uniquely perfect! Paul continues in the following verse, twenty-four: "'Yet God, in his grace, freely makes us right in his sight. He did this through Christ Jesus when he freed us from the penalty for our sins." In a free, gracious act of love, God offers this to all the imperfect images, because we must be perfect in order to dwell in loving relationship with the perfect God who is perfect. (By nature, a being who is perfect has perfect standards; therefore, our perfection is required for us to be in relationship with the God who is perfectly perfect in and of himself.)

In the third chapter of the Gospel of John, Jesus says God does this because he loves the world. Furthermore, Jesus says there is no striving or work required to attain this necessary perfection ("righteousness" is the biblical term). For good reason, John 3:16 is a very popular sentence in a fascinating, poetic book about God. It says this: "For God so loved the world that he gave his one and only Son, that whoever believes in him shall not perish but have eternal life." It's an amazing statement, but it is the sentences that come just before it that intrigue me even more in a context such as Idealism, so let's look at the scene in which this statement is set.

Jesus is speaking with a very religious man named Nicodemus. Jesus, as a good teacher, knows he needs to give Nicodemus a point of reference or comparison for this gift of salvation. Ironically Nicodemus is what we might call a Religious Theistic Idealist; he is part of a Jewish sect called the Pharisees, and Pharisees were known for their strict observance of God's Law. For most of his life, Nicodemus has been caught up in trying to make himself morally and religiously perfect to please "Yahweh" (God the Father). Nicodemus is unaware he is speaking with God in the Flesh, who is lovingly and relationally offering him the Good News of righteousness and perfection, attained by Grace, not through striving and personal works of sacrifice and purity. Before Jesus makes the incredible offer of salvation (John 3:16), he sets the scene.

Now you need to understand that both Jesus and Nicodemus have incredible knowledge of the Old Testament—they've memorized it! Jesus could have picked anything in the Old Testament to compare salvation so he could have referred to the parting of the Red Sea; the blood on the doorposts in Egypt; the ram sacrificed for Isaac; the falling of the walls of Jericho; the fire from heaven with Elijah... Rather than any of these, Jesus picks the story of the snake on a pole. Here is what he says: "14 Just as Moses lifted up the snake in the wilderness, so the Son of Man must be lifted up,15 that everyone who believes may have eternal life in him. 16 For God so loved the world that he gave his one and only Son, that whoever believes in him shall not perish but have eternal life. 17 For God did not send his Son into the world to condemn the world, but to save the world through him."

The snake on a pole incident is told in Numbers chapter 29. The Israelites were being bitten by poisonous snakes in the wilderness (they were not yet in the Promised Land.) The people were dying from these snake bites; they needed salvation from them. Rather than God eradicating all the snakes (which makes logical sense to me), God told Moses to fashion a bronze snake and put it on a pole. Whoever looked at the snake on the pole was saved from the deadly snake bites. Salvation from death was accomplished by a simple glance.

We, too, are poisoned. The poison of imperfection and sin is all around us and in us, coursing through our communities and our bloodstream. According to Jesus, salvation from this toxic situation is a glance at the Fullness of Reality giving himself up to restore us to our full selves and to a loving relationship with him. Jesus tells Nicodemus that salvation is a glance, not a long striving of self-righteousness; it is righteousness (perfection) offered as a gift; it is salvation through meaningful, trusting, hopeful eye contact with the Living God—who was sitting right in front of him! I wonder if their eyes met in the starlight in that moment.

If Nicodemus were a Buddhist, meeting Jesus on another rooftop in another conversation, he would have to consider this teacher's profound message. The invitation here is not to let go of self and attain perfect union with God—as God—through suffering and striving; the invitation is to retain and become oneself by ceasing to strive, by receiving the gift of perfection—becoming the perfected version of yourself in loving relationship as yourself with

God. The eightfold path of the Buddha and the path of loving grace offered by Christ are two very different paths built from two very different trust lists. Remember Elisha's servant, afraid of the physical army surrounding the city? When his eyes were opened to the reality of the far greater spiritual army, he no longer feared. The perception of reality he chose to trust did not change the Reality, but it affected him! In the same way, the perception of reality you choose to trust as true will not change the Truth of Prime Reality. But it will change how you feel about your understanding of reality and your daily decisions within Reality. When the Light of Christ is turned off in your trust list, authentic, life-giving, divine Love and Grace are left powerless as an influence in your life.

CHAPTER 20
MATERIALISM

In the light of Materialism, the physical world is valued and honored. Actions done in the physical world have effect; the consequences can be seen and felt and observed. This is an important revelation, for it gives importance to what we experience through our senses. The beauty and goodness of what is seen, touched, tasted, and smelled is real, is true. Our lives matter here and now. The now matters; and material preferences matter; and "matter matters." As my friend Bishop Stewart Ruch says, "If I like my coffee with cream and sugar and you like yours black, both are valid choices, and our individuality can be celebrated." Much of life is relative and simply preference, like the smell of roses and the flavor of ice cream (though that is of utmost importance). When we hold someone's hand, see someone's smile, hear the sound of a loved one's voice, or taste a delicious meal, we have experienced something real. Furthermore, our perception of and desire for material distinctions are significant and vital because they reveal the desire for autonomy and individuality. The earth, with all its ever-transforming, varied beauty, should be cared for and honored. The creative, unique makeup of each material thing, both organic and inorganic, is to be celebrated as the epitome of existential reality.

And this is where the shadow of materialism begins, for if matter is all that matters and nothing outside the material world exists or matters, this has enormous ramifications. Feelings and emotions then are nothing more than chemical reactions, as are rational thoughts, intellectual assertions, or personal opinions. The longings we have for relationship and unity and connection are not actually real beyond chemical bonds and electrical impulses, and there can be no such thing as authentic free will (and therefore, no real sense of autonomy and responsibility). All that is "real" are the physical interactions caused by chemical reactions, firing randomly and yet semi-predictably, but totally outside of human control.

As this book is being penned, humanity is on the brink of creating self-piloting cars and aircraft. In the foreseeable future, a vehicle could drive "itself" without a self inside it. The vehicle would be propelled by an internal (yet dependent) energy source; it would completely react to input and output of information received and transmitted through sensors; and this information would be processed through a brain of sorts, a computer which processes this information and reacts to the environment and makes predetermined choices based off of preset and "learned or stored" information. The device will appear to be making choices, will look as if it is deciding what to do next; however, people who know how these devices work would adamantly argue that the device is not genuinely choosing anything freely; it cannot go beyond what the program allows. If a child runs in front of the car, it will stop simply because it has been programmed to stop when anything gets in its path. Essentially, the child is no different from the vehicle than a runaway shopping cart. It has made no moral decision in the process.

If someone only trusts in the material realm as really real; if someone believes all we are is an amalgamation of electrons and matter—then we are no different in our essence than a computer or battery-operated toy; all that is different is the stuff of which we are made and the complexity of the device. Therefore, there is no sense of freedom or control. It takes a being within the shell of the car or airplane, in connection with the device and with the ability to have some sense of control over the device, for there to be any real essence of freedom and choice related to the driver or pilot and the car or plane. Theists refer to this pilot/driver as the soul or spirit of a person. It is the immaterial driver of the body; it is in connection with the body but is not the body (as seen at death). For a theist, the human soul is individual and unique. Each body is connected to a soul, but the soul is not limited to the substance of the body. Smarter people than I have written plenty on this issue. I simply offer an illustration of what the idea of the human soul can mean when we view it in the lights of both Monism and Theism: If each human has a unique soul in connection with a particular body, and if each human invites the unifying Spirit of God to indwell his/her body to live in relation with, not as, that human soul in that particular body, the ramifications are incredible. The presence of two souls inside the physical finiteness of a body allows for individuality, uniqueness, connectedness, unity, distinction, autonomy, love, and freedom! It provides for the stuff of real, meaningful life. When the lights of Theism and Monism and the spiritual are turned off, however, real living—real life!—is turned off. We are left merely with chemical reactions and the appearance of life.

If you take the idea of complete Materialism to its ultimate end, life becomes meaningless and without purpose. An authentic atheist will wholeheartedly embrace this concept; interestingly, though, few are genuine in their understanding of the natural consequences of trusting materialism. Here are a few of these consequences: What we think of as our "self" ceases to exist when the heart stops beating and the chemical reactions stop firing. Reality is restricted to the material world, and this material world holds no inherent sense of any real objective standard of right and wrong; it can't because there is nothing other than the material to allow for any real objectivity. Morality has, therefore, no real meaning. Right and wrong, beauty and goodness, truth and honor are nothing more than concepts, determined by individuals or groups of individuals and their existential perspective on reality. If Materialism is the whole truth, Good and Evil are arbitrary; there is no set standard, no objectivity. This means that, though there can be preferences, there can be no evil and no good.

To illustrate this issue with my students, I ask them each to draw an inch on a piece of paper. "Who has the right inch?" I then ask. Without a ruler, can we determine that? Do we simply pick one student's "inch" and use that as a standard until another student argues forcefully and skillfully enough that their inch is actually better? Until we pull out a ruler with its determined, absolute, authoritative, objective inch, any "inch" we draw is arbitrary. Of course, any materialist who claims a sense of objectivity for morality will do it on these premises. They will assert that we have all agreed on our "inch" as humanity, or better yet, our genes have decided what works best to perpetuate the genome. I find it rare to find a modern materialist who will clearly articulate the actual absurdity of modern human morality for the Materialist Trust List. Albert Camus in his work The Stranger and Friedrich Nietzsche with his piece, Thus Spake Zarathustra, were at least honest and open about this natural consequence of killing an objective authority for morality. Objective, authentic meaning and morality die when God literally and conceptually dies. I do not have any issues with Nietzsche when he states that God died; I believe that happened 2000 years ago on the cross at Calvary just outside of Jerusalem. Nietzsche's real stab at Theism occurs when he states that "God remains dead."

This point can be further illustrated by a letter I wrote to the late atheist Christopher Hitchens in response to his bestseller God is not Great: How Religion Poisons Everything. I had already encountered the trust list of the famous Oxford atheist Richard Dawkins (after filling his pockets by purchasing three of his books and thoroughly unpacking his devoted trust in probability; the scientific method of observation and theorizing; and the unlimited potential of infinite time). While I appreciated Dawkins' honesty—at least in the title of chapter four of his book The God Delusion: "Why There Almost Certainly Is Not a God," I was a bit disappointed at his inauthenticity in not mentioning the natural consequences of his beliefs, such as the absurdity of life without meaning, morality, autonomy, and free will. Therefore, when several people told me Hitchens' book was quite compelling, I had high hopes that it would answer some of the questions I had after reading Dawkins' works.

I can honestly say I loved reading God is not Great; it was life transforming for me as a Christian. Hitchens is an intriguing writer who crafts arguments with energy and vigor. He does a smashing job talking about the atrocities and abuses of religion. I found myself cheering out loud in angry solidarity while reading his excellent description of the horrors of slavery; the perpetual violations of women in the name of God; the pettiness of denominational divisiveness over rituals; and devious exploitation of the farcical miraculous (his choice of the word "tawdry" was brilliant). On top of all of this, I simply love the yellow cover and the audacity of the title. It is compelling—but unfortunately inaccurate. I wanted to use the book in my class but knew the title would get in the way, and I wasn't sure what to do about that.

It came to me one night as I gazed out at the Chicago skyline from high up in the Wit Hotel. Some generous and kind friends of ours had gifted my family with a night in this hotel, and my twins and wife were comfortably sleeping in the warm city glow. It was the third watch of the night; I had just finished Hitchens' book; and I was still up, thinking about it. Then it hit me: I knew how I could use the book in my class. I grabbed my copy of the book and a Sharpie marker. It all became perfectly clear when I retitled the book; It was the same message Nietzsche had sent the world so many years before. My new cover read, "God's Followers are Not That Great: How the Abuse of Religion Poisons Everything." Like a dislocated-then-relocated shoulder, the whole of the book fell into place. I had a new friend in Christopher Hitchens. He had not written about Religion or God. He had written about how the misguided, ego-driven, selfish, narcissistic, short-sighted, dimwitted followers of God, like me, have misrepresented the True God and how we so-called devotees have misused and abused religion in God's name. Hitchens did not write about how grace and love poison everything. He did not write about the toxic abuse of forgiveness and mercy. He did not write about how loving, authentic, healthy, life-changing and life-giving supernatural signs, wonders, miracles, and encounters with the relational and personal God have ruined and destroyed the individuals who truly experienced them. He did not write about a loving God who saves the world at his own personal expense and then offers it as a free gift to all of humanity. Nor did he write about how this God desires deep, beautiful harmony and mutual honor amongst all people and his amazing creation. He did not write about a God who "delight(s)" in us, who "rejoice(s) over (us) with singing" Zephaniah 3:17. Nor did he do justice to the compassionate, generous, and compelling character and nature of Jesus as found in the Gospels.

I quickly wrote out my letter to Hitchens. The aim was twofold. If I were to use his book as a text in my class, I wanted permission to pass out Sharpies so my students could retitle his book to be a more accurate representation of what he wrote. (I doubted that the board of trustees at my little Christian school would let me use it with the current title.) Second, I wanted to know if he had published any writing on the absurdity of life, the capricious nature of living without free will, and the absurdity of morality. In the letter, I mentioned my frustration on this matter.

The tension I felt compelled to address with Mr. Hitchens was his glaring lack of acknowledgment of the horrors of authentic Materialistic morality. He did a great job of pointing out the abuses of religion—for which I applaud him. But he is only able to do this because of the overt and apparent standards for morality that "religion" has—many of which he agrees with. He opposes slavery because of his desire to champion freedom of the human will, which is ironic because authentic atheism adheres to the notion that humans do not even have a will, let alone a free one, as Sam Harris finally admitted in one of his latest books on atheism. Hitchens ridicules fake miracles, not realizing his argument is ridiculous, that the very word "fake" implies there must be something real to be counterfeited: truth is necessary for a lie to exist. Hitchens talks about how immoral patriarchal, domineering religion can be in its abuses towards women—and yet neglects to address the standard the God of the Hebrew Bible himself set by making women of equal value to men as equally made in the image of God. Women thus are to be treated with the same honor as men as half of the representation of the nature of God to all of humanity. He also failed to address the fact that true atheism has no objective standard of honoring or valuing women, and I am left to wonder about the foundation on which he bases his authority for the humane treatment of any human.

Finally and most importantly, Hitchens rails about the abuses of morality in religion with all of the bullying, terrorism, torture, and even killing that at times happens. Admittedly humans, using the name of God, have committed some of the most unspeakably horrific atrocities ever committed on this planet. And that is my main point: Hitchens can only call these actions horrifying and abusive if there is a real standard, and the very religions he despises provides the standard. I call terrorism an abuse of religion because there is a standard set by God to love and forgive my enemies, not terrorize and torture them. Jesus even says I am not supposed to hate my enemies simply because of what it does to my heart. When Hitchens sees terrorist activities, he notices something is inherently wrong only because there is a God-Given Objective Standard (which exists even if he does not acknowledge it), and Hitchens recognizes that terrorism is a deviation from it.

This is also understood when a Christian church makes signs and statements that say "God Hates Homosexuals." Again, this is a blatant ABUSE of religion because of this standard of morality: God loves all people. This is seen in John 3:16 and in many other verses throughout Scripture. There is blatant abuse because of an objective standard. Thus, that church and terrorists are morally wrong according to the God-given Objective Standard. My question for Hitchens is if he has considered the potential horrors of atheistic, un-objective morality. What would we do in a world in which there is no objective standard for morality? We would usher in a world with no abuses of morality because there would be no standard to abuse or from which to deviate. If Hitchens got his way and all religions were dismantled, thus removing all standards for morality, then he would necessarily have no right to be upset about crimes against his personal preferences of morality. I am more concerned about a world in which nothing can be an abuse of morality because there is no acknowledged standard of morality than I am about the world where we can all point out the glaring violations of morality based on the Natural Law of morality that God has embedded in each of us, hidden in the created order, and even shared with humans in the special revelation of his Word.

In Mere Christianity C.S. Lewis has some very insightful commentary on this issue. It is helpful to keep in mind that Lewis was a staunch atheist for over 15 years of his adult life before he accepted Christianity. He says:

> "My argument against God was that the universe seemed so cruel and unjust. But how had I got this idea of just and unjust? A man does not call a line crooked unless he has some idea of a straight line. What was I comparing this universe with when I called it unjust? If the whole show was bad and senseless from A to Z, so to speak, why did I, who was supposed to be part of the show, find myself in such violent reaction against it? A man feels wet when he falls into water because man is not a water animal: a fish would not feel wet.
>
> "Of course I could have given up my idea of justice by saying it was nothing but a private idea of my own. But if I did that, then my argument against God collapsed too—for the argument depended on saying that the world was really unjust, not simply that it did not happen to please my private fancies. Thus in the very act of trying to prove that God did not exist—in other words, that the whole of reality was senseless—I found I was forced to assume that one part of reality—namely my idea of justice—was full of sense.
>
> "Consequently atheism turns out to be too simple. If the whole universe has no meaning, we should never have found out that it has no meaning: just as, if there were no light in the

universe and therefore no creatures with eyes, we should never know it was dark. Dark would be without meaning."

Conclusion: The light of materialism gives value to the physical world. It declares it real. This is a truth to hold onto while we acknowledge that many other answers presented by materialism are shadowy, insubstantial, and do not adequately answer the deep questions of the human heart. If you follow materialism far enough, in fact, the shadows of materialism ironically begin to negate even the light it reveals. For we want life and relationships to hold meaning and purpose; we want love to be real; we want humans to be held accountable for their choices; we want to be able to say gross injustice—actions such as rape and murder and child abuse—is wrong and evil; many of us want to believe there is a spirit within us that continues after physical death. Every human I have ever met has agreed that we all have a sense of justice deep within us that makes us desire all to be well for all people, yet all of this becomes absurd when we turn off the lights of the other worldviews.

CHAPTER 21
MONISM

Pure monists say we are all united and connected, and quite frankly this is true: the entire universe is connected materially (molecularly and through light) and even supernaturally/spiritually. This means all humanity is far more connected than it is divided; humans are connected with each other, just as they are connected with nature and animals. The bright light of Monism offers a beacon of hope and motivation to seek unity and harmony with all of life—with all of reality! All, together, make up reality, and all are both material and spiritual. Monism values both the material and spiritual world by saying they are one, a unified whole manifesting itself in two different ways. Reality is like a person with both a front and a back. The front of a person may look entirely unlike his/her back, but this person is still only one human, both sides work together making the whole person. Reality, therefore, can be found in both the physical, material world and the mysterious spiritual world. Both have meaning; both have purpose. There is a connection to be pursued, and it can and should be pursued through physical reality as well as through spiritual reality, for the two are not separate but united. One affects the other; one is connected to the other, again, like a person and like a coin with two sides. Spirituality is embedded in material reality, thus making beauty possible. Materialism is embedded in spirituality, thus giving spirituality expression and shape. Matter matters; spiritual reality matters; everything matters. Thoughts and actions completed in the material world are also affecting the spiritual world and vice versa.

But this light by itself leads directly to the shadows. For if the entirety of everything—together, connected and united—is "god," then, like pure materialism, there is no absolute objective standard, nor can there be an objective absolute standard that determines good or evil, truth or falsity. As mentioned earlier, Materialism and Idealism can and should be considered monistic, in that there is only the belief in "one" reality as prime reality; thus there is no option for the "other" to exist to create any objectivity, relationship, or value. If everything is god, then we have, in effect, lost God. God loses identity, and humans lose theirs as well. When humans cease to have a unique, definitive self, there is no basis for a relationship; we are all part of a waterlogged watercolor painting that never takes shape, that has no one painting it—at least no one outside the painting. Rather, everything in the painting is painting. Lewis says this about monism, which he calls pantheism:

> "Pantheists usually believe that God, so to speak, animates the universe as you animate your body: that the universe almost is God, so that if it did not exist He would not exist either, and anything you find in the universe is a part of God. The Christian idea is quite different. Christians think God invented and made the universe—like a man making a picture or composing a tune. A painter is not a picture, and he does not die if his picture is destroyed. You may say, 'He's put a lot of himself into it,' but you only mean that all its beauty and interest has come out of his head. His skill is not in the picture in the same way that it is in his head, or even in his hands. I expect you to see how this difference between Pantheists and Christians hangs together with the other one. If you do not take the distinction between good and bad very seriously, then it is easy to say that anything you find in this world is a part of God. But, of course, if you think some things really bad, and God really good, then you cannot talk like that. You must believe that God is separate from the world and that some of the things we see in it are contrary to His will. Confronted with a cancer or a slum the Pantheist can say, 'If you could only see it from the divine point of view, you would realize that this also is God.' The Christian replies, 'Don't talk damned nonsense.'(*)
>
> [*] One listener complained of the word damned as frivolous swearing. But I mean exactly what I say—nonsense that is damned is under God's curse, and will (apart from God's grace) lead those who believe it to eternal death."

In pure Monism, purpose is lost; distinction is lost; relationship is lost; right and wrong are lost. The Star Wars movies are good examples of this. Please keep in mind that I love the Star Wars movies. I believe all great stories point us to the True Great Story we are in, and these are great stories! However, I am aware that when we watch Star Wars, we impose our view of morality on it; therefore, the Jedi are the "good guys" and Darth Vader and the Empire are the "bad." But there is nothing objective, no overarching Authoritative Being or Ideal standard in the movie's monistic viewpoint that determines this. The Force, in everything and in everyone, is amoral. It makes no distinctions and sets no standards and has no ultimate purpose. Viewers often see Anakin's turn away from the Jedi and toward the Empire as a choice for evil, but the movie does not necessarily present it that way. It is merely a choice of preference. I remember watching the scene on the river of lava when Anakin is confronted by Obi-Wan Kenobi about his choice of loyalty. When Anakin is cautioned that he is turning from good toward evil, he argues that he simply sees it differently: "From my point of view," he says, "the Jedi are evil." I jumped up and danced around the room at this point, exclaiming, "He actually says it out loud!" My nephew laughed at the hilarity of watching movies with his crazy uncle. Yet we later talked about how, in the context of the universe and world view of Star Wars, Anakin—or any character—is free to make that choice; there is no ultimate consequence, for the Force may be powerful, but it is not concerned with right and wrong, only perspective.

You may be asking, like many of my students, "What's the difference between materialism and monism?" It's a good question. The distinction lies in the belief in spiritual power, but even though monism holds that humans are both material and spiritual beings, monism, like materialism, holds no human ultimately accountable for the choices they make. In both, humans are free to make whatever "choices" suit them best. (And for both, ironically, this so-called "choice" is merely the perception of choice, since there is no real self-direction in either of these world views.) Since there is no God to submit to, with a will that determines good and evil, then each human's will is, essentially, the will of god. The end results—as seen in lives lived completely by monistic or materialistic principles—seem very similar.

Chesterton quips on this in his wily ways in Orthodoxy, Suicide of Thought:

> "To sum up our contention so far, we may say that the most characteristic current philosophies have not only a touch of mania, but a touch of suicidal mania. The mere questioner has

knocked his head against the limits of human thought; and cracked it. This is what makes so futile the warnings of the orthodox and the boasts of the advanced about the dangerous boyhood of free thought. What we are looking at is not the boyhood of free thought; it is the old age and ultimate dissolution of free thought. It is vain for bishops and pious bigwigs to discuss what dreadful things will happen if wild skepticism runs its course. It has run its course. It is vain for eloquent atheists to talk of the great truths that will be revealed if once we see free thought begin. We have seen it end. It has no more questions to ask; it has questioned itself. You cannot call up any wilder vision than a city in which men ask themselves if they have any selves. You cannot fancy a more skeptical world than that in which men doubt if there is a world."

"We have no more questions left to ask. We have looked for questions in the darkest corners and on the wildest peaks. We have found all the questions that can be found. It is time we gave up looking for questions and began looking for answers."

CHAPTER 22
RELIGIOUS THEISM

Now we come to religious theism, the worldview that includes, but is not limited to, the religions of Islam, Judaism, Christianity, and tribal religions that worship a Creator and The Great Spirit. I have made my view of Christ very clear by this point, so I understand readers may assume I will see more light in this worldview than in the others. After all, I clearly am not approaching this study as a materialist, monist, or idealist so my view of "light" and "dark" will be biased from a theistic perspective. However, I contend that Christ, not a religion, is the fullness of reality, so I see lights on and lights off in this worldview as well.

Shining in the light of religious theism is the idea that there is a Perfect Ideal: God. As in Idealism, God is complete goodness, truth, and beauty; therefore, God is the standard. All attempts at goodness, beauty, and truth are measured against God; and this standard draws a clear line between good and evil. The God of religious theism, though, is a Creator, a Creator who created both spiritual and material reality. Both are real; both are valued. This truth is much like what is revealed in Monism, but there is a significant difference: the created spiritual and material realities are distinct from God. This light illuminates the deep feeling we humans have that there is a right way to act and a wrong way—and this "way" comes from outside us. C. S. Lewis puts it like this: humans

> "have this curious idea that they ought to behave in a certain way, and cannot get rid of it..." and this leads to the idea that there is "Something which is directing the universe, and which appears in (them) as a law urging (them) to do right and making (them) responsible and uncomfortable when (they) do wrong." (8 and 25 in MC). Religious theism sheds light on these ideas held deep within us. This, too, is similar to what is revealed by the light of Idealism, but the unique light of religious theism illuminates the distinction of God from creation, as not just a creator but a relational being. The goal for humanity is still to become perfect, to become like God,

> but in religious theism, humans do not become God or even a part of God. They remain unique and individual, with both material and spiritual "sides" of their being, and God remains God. The God of religious theism is not indistinct and vague but has personality and being. Furthermore, as God's creation, we humans have a standard and a purpose: to live up to God's perfection, to be in right relationship with God and other humans."

For this section of my course, I have my students put down this text and pick up a copy of Mere Christianity by C. S. Lewis. If you have not read his book yet, now is a great time to do so. They are asked to read and annotate the first book, approximately thirty pages. The companion guidebook to this textbook has several pages and additional resources to help you navigate a close reading of Lewis' writing. Lewis opens with powerful statements, taking on the moral argument for the existence of God. These pages contain one of the most succinct and eloquent apologetics ever written on this topic. This is particularly effective because he accomplishes his task without any mention of the Bible or Jesus. It echoes the apostle Paul's declaration in the opening paragraphs of Romans: 'For ever since the world was created, people have seen the earth and sky. Through everything God made, they can clearly see his invisible qualities—his eternal power and divine nature. So they have no excuse for not knowing God.' (1:20).

Quite possibly the most essential aspect of theism is represented in the painting of creation in the Sistine Chapel, in which Adam and God are pictured as recognizably human figures. They are positioned a short distance from each other, and each has one hand outstretched toward the other, but they are not quite touching. God's pointer finger is extended as if Adam has just sprung forth from it. I know that brilliant art historians and critics like my good friend Nate Leman could go on for pages about the meaning embedded within that painting, but my simple focus here is the "space" between Adam's and God's fingers and the fact that Adam and God look very similar, that God is presented as a being like Adam. Sure, Adam is in the image of God; Adam is remarkably "like God," but contrariwise, God is "like Adam"—God is like us. Before you throw this book and me in the fire, just consider the profundity of that statement—" he made them male and female, in the image of God they were made." If Adam and Eve are in the image of God, then God is at least on some level represented in the image of Adam and Eve. Otherwise being in the image of God would not be a true statement. The value of being in the image of God and being like God, but not God, and being like other humans but not other humans is that we all exist distinct from each other enough to not be each other.

As mentioned earlier, all the other worldviews are monistic in essence; theism is the only worldview with a trust in the distinct "otherness" of beings. Without this distinction of Theism—that "space" between the fingers in the Sistine Chapel—we lose our distinction and diversity and simply become extensions of God, like marionettes or extra appendages; we lose self and slip into the one "self" of God. Thus, theism is the only worldview in which relationship, free will, love, and value can actually exist with any real meaning. Yet this alone is not enough. Without the truth and light of Monism, humans would be literally distinct from each other and God—actually separated from God, who is the author and sustainer of life, particularly eternal life.

Just as in the other worldviews, the light turned off in theism is in many ways related to the light turned on. The understanding of God, of God's objective morality, can either make religious theism hellish or beautiful. Without the light of idealism, religious theism does not have to have love and goodness at the core of its objective morality. Without love and goodness, religious theism is abusive and controlling, even terrifying. Though we have that "curious idea" of right and wrong deep within us, without a concrete, accurate "definition" (theology) or "picture or image" of God, our view of right and wrong—and therefore of God—can be terribly skewed. We can "create" our own individual god, who approves what we approve, likes who and what we like, and dislikes who and what we don't; and then religiously we can use Godlike authority to condone or condemn others based on our version of God's standard for behavior and even value. This hellish abuse naturally compels authors like Hitchens to write books about the abuses of religion. Without the light of unity (shed powerfully and profoundly by monism), religious theism creates us-versus-them attitudes that celebrate distinction and differences, that use rules and moralism to create an "in" crowd—and an "out" one. In Christianity alone, this has produced thousands upon thousands of religious denominations—and this is the faith that claims to follow Christ, who prayed that his followers would be one. Islam and Judaism have similar divisive denominational issues.

Without the idea of unity, religious theists are free to create a god who is not concerned with the good of all people, with the good of all creation. For many religious theists, God does not have to be the God of all; he can simply be a god who is for one particular group, who is against all others. Without the essential light of materialism, the god created by religious theism is not that concerned with the here and now and the physical state of people and the world. Religious theism unlit by materialism is free to focus only on a later existence in a spiritual realm; it can justify this focus and treat it as if it is more important than the material. People who follow this kind of spiritually-focused theism tend to think that the most important thing—perhaps even the only thing—is getting to heaven and saving souls for heaven; they forget, or have not heard, or don't believe that God came to earth and dwelt in a physical body.

Without the other three lights, religious theism tends to create a god who is perhaps the "ideal" for a particular individual or group but who is not the Ideal for all, who is not complete, absolute, untainted Truth, Beauty, and Goodness. I will now speak for Christians and not necessarily the other theistic religions. It can be easy to forget that "God so loved the world." It can be easy to forget that Christ's birth was announced as "Good News for all the people…" I will now speak for all theistic religions and not necessarily the just Christians. When religious theism is taken to the extreme, particularly related to the truth of distinction and personal autonomy, it has, primarily, set aside the true God; created a human concept of a god controlled by a religion; established a rigid moral code; and embossed the entire system with the stamp of religious authority, a powerful stamp indeed.

If you picked up this book as a religious theist, be it as a follower of Islam, Judaism, or Christianity, you must ask yourself where you have potentially turned off the lights of the truths held by idealism, materialism, and monism. In what ways have you or your "ism" created a false god and a misuse of religion and religious authority? There is much more to write on this topic, but that is for another book.

CHAPTER 23
THE PARADOX

This was the big fact about Christian ethics; the discovery of the new balance. Paganism had been like a pillar of marble, upright because proportioned with symmetry. Christianity was like a huge and ragged and romantic rock, which, though it sways on its pedestal at a touch, yet, because its exaggerated excrescences exactly balance each other, is enthroned there for a thousand years. In a Gothic cathedral the columns were all different, but they were all necessary. Every support seemed an accidental and fantastic support; every buttress was a flying buttress. So in Christendom apparent accidents balanced. Becket wore a hair shirt under his gold and crimson, and there is much to be said for the combination; for Becket got the benefit of the hair shirt while the people in the street got the benefit of the crimson and gold. It is at least better than the manner of the modern millionaire, who has the black and the drab outwardly for others, and the gold next to his heart. But the balance was not always in one man's body as in Becket's; the balance was often distributed over the whole body of Christendom. Because a man prayed and fasted on the Northern snows, flowers could be flung at his festival in the Southern cities; and because fanatics drank water on the sands of Syria, men could still drink cider in the orchards of England. This is what makes Christendom at once so much more perplexing and so much more interesting than the Pagan empire; just as Amiens Cathedral is not better but more interesting than the Parthenon.... We will make an equipoise out of these excesses.

Last and most important, it is exactly this which explains what is so inexplicable to all the modern critics of the history of Christianity. I mean the monstrous wars about small points of theology, the earthquakes of emotion about a gesture or a word. It was only a matter of an inch; but an inch is everything when you are balancing. The Church could not afford to swerve a hair's breadth on some things if she was to continue her great and daring experiment of the irregular equilibrium. Once let one idea become less powerful, and some other idea would become too powerful. It was no flock of sheep the Christian shepherd was leading, but a herd of bulls and tigers, of terrible ideals and devouring doctrines, each one of them strong enough to turn to a false religion and lay waste the world. Remember that the Church went in specifically for dangerous ideas; she was a lion tamer. The idea of birth through a Holy Spirit, of the death of a divine being, of the forgiveness of sins, or the fulfillment of prophecies, are ideas which, anyone can see, need but a touch to turn them into something blasphemous or ferocious. The smallest link was let drop by the artificers of the Mediterranean, and the lion of ancestral pessimism burst his chain in the forgotten forests of the north. Of these theological equalisations I have to speak afterwards. Here it is enough to notice that if some small mistake were made in doctrine, huge blunders might be made in human happiness. A sentence phrased wrong about the nature of symbolism would have broken all the best statues in Europe. A slip in the definitions might stop all the dances; might wither all the Christmas trees or break all the Easter eggs.

G.K. Chesterton
Orthodoxy Ch. 6 Paradoxes of Christianity p101-102

It is human default to deny the lights of any worldview other than our own. We are, in many ways, more comfortable living in the shadows, where we assume we have all the light there is. Many of us have never been directly invited to consider that more light is available to us. But when we become aware there is more light when sparks of that light are revealed to us, we are faced with a decision: do we begin the arduous and often painful journey toward the light or do we simply stay put?

This journey into the full light can be long, and it is sometimes almost cyclical—we feel as if we are learning the same "lessons" again and again, but each time "around" there is a greater fullness and depth to what we learn and experience. Many teachers, philosophers, and writers are starting to use a helix as an effective metaphor for this concept because a helix is linear and cyclical at the same time. This journey will never allow us to feel as if we have arrived. We will always be learning, always be growing, always be stepping into a little more light. This is partly why I fashioned this book as a Shakespearean play, for in a sense the story does not end when the curtain drops. Shakespeare's stories and characters are so close to real-life stories and real-life characters that we understand the play represents a slice of the story of life; the characters represent you, me, us. People continue on with their lives after one "story" is finished; they embark on new stories that are also continuations of their old stories, that are part of their overall stories, that are part of the tremendous Eternal Love Story already written and simultaneously being written by God.

If this is what you choose, to open your eyes and ears and heart to the Great Adventure Story, to become a pilgrim on an ever-brightening journey to a holy place, you must embrace the idea of paradox. For reality is paradoxical. It is both material and spiritual; it is united but distinct; it is objective yet relative, and it is brutally impersonal and intimately personal.

This is the power of paradox. This is the truth and power of mystery. All worldviews, religions, isms, and ways have, at their cores, a deep sense of mystery and wonder. If you continue to press into them and ask questions of them, all of them (even materialism) will lead you to a place of paradox, and if you enter fully into this place of paradox, you are forced to surrender your belief that you have everything figured out, that you have all the answers. And this place of surrender and acceptance is a good place; it's a place where you can begin to look for Truth. Chesterton knew this. He implies that the power of paradox is what unlocked the truth and freedom of Christianity for him. I know many people will say paradox is a wimpy alternative to seeking "real truth." They often tell me I am just giving up my quest for true understanding, but I believe paradox is not the end of my understanding; it is the place where my understanding begins to germinate into what Richard Rohr calls "endless knowability." In his weekly summary of his daily devotions in August 2016, which focused on Paradox, Rohr stated:

- "The binary, dualistic mind cannot deal with contradictions, paradox, or mystery, all of which are at the heart of religion. *(Sunday)*
- The very nature of spiritual truth is that it is paradoxical. *(Monday)*
- The times where we meet or reckon with our contradictions are often turning points, opportunities to enter into the deeper mystery of God or, alternatively, to evade the mystery of God. *(Tuesday)*

• If you hold both sides seriously, that is the space in which you can grow morally, in understanding what really matters. That is the space in which you can go deep and learn mystery—which is endlessly knowability. *(Wednesday)*

• The third way is not balancing or even eliminating the opposites, but holding the opposites, as Jesus did on the cross. To live inside this space of creative tension is the very character of faith, hope, and love. *(Thursday)*

• [This third Christ-like option] (which Rohr calls the "Third Force" energy) is overcoming seeming opposites by uncovering a reconciling third that is bigger than both of the parts and doesn't exclude either of them. *(Friday)"*

Chesterton writes an entire chapter on paradox. It is aptly titled "The Paradoxes of Christianity." Here is its opening paragraph:

> "The real trouble with this world of ours is not that it is an unreasonable world, nor even that it is a reasonable one. The commonest kind of trouble is that it is nearly reasonable, but not quite. Life is not an illogicality, yet it is a trap for logicians. It looks just a little more mathematical and regular than it is; its exactitude is obvious, but its inexactitude is hidden; its wildness lies in wait. I give one coarse instance of what I mean. Suppose some mathematical creature from the moon were to reckon up the human body; he would at once see that the essential thing about it was that it was duplicate. A man is two men, he on the right exactly resembling him on the left. Having noted that there was an arm on the right and one on the left, a leg on the right and one on the left, he might go further and still find on each side the same number of fingers, the same number of toes, twin eyes, twin ears, twin nostrils, and even twin lobes of the brain. At last, he would take it as a law; and then, where he found a heart on one side, would deduce that there was another heart on the other. And just then, where he most felt he was right, he would be wrong."

Chesterton points out the essential need for paradox to understand fundamental human reality even related to a nonreligious general and secular virtue like courage. He writes,

> "But granted that we have all to keep a balance, the real interest comes in with the question of how that balance can be kept. That was the problem which Paganism tried to solve: that

was the problem which I think Christianity solved and solved in a very strange way.

"Paganism declared that virtue was in a balance; Christianity declared it was in a conflict: the collision of two passions apparently opposite. Of course, they were not really inconsistent; but they were such that it was hard to hold simultaneously. Let us follow for a moment the clue of the martyr and the suicide, and take the case of courage. No quality has ever so much addled the brains and tangled the definitions of merely rational sages. Courage is almost a contradiction in terms. It means a strong desire to live taking the form of a readiness to die. 'He that will lose his life, the same shall save it,' is not a piece of mysticism for saints and heroes. It is a piece of everyday advice for sailors or mountaineers. It might be printed in an Alpine guide or a drill book. This paradox is the whole principle of courage; even of quite earthly or quite brutal courage. A man cut off by the sea may save his life if he will risk it on the precipice.

"He can only get away from death by continually stepping within an inch of it. A soldier surrounded by enemies, if he is to cut his way out, needs to combine a strong desire for living with a strange carelessness about dying. He must not merely cling to life, for then he will be a coward, and will not escape. He must not merely wait for death, for then he will be a suicide, and will not escape. He must seek his life in a spirit of furious indifference to it; he must desire life like water and yet drink death like wine. No philosopher, I fancy, has ever expressed this romantic riddle with adequate lucidity, and I certainly have not done so. But Christianity has done more: it has marked the limits of it in the awful graves of the suicide and the hero, showing the distance between him who dies for the sake of living and him who dies for the sake of dying."

For our purposes here we need to connect Chesterton's ideas with the tensions of the four worldviews and the various lights in the chandelier. Paradox is not the seeming contradiction and the mysterious truth of a clever statement. Paradox is what happens when we find two polarities in reality that seem to be in conflict, but both of them are true; thus, rather than picking one of the opposing truths and disregarding the other, we must hold both conflicting truths in tension with each other. In my approach to worldview, I am not proposing some vague pluralism where all the views are simultaneously true and are actually one mushy "truth" which is not a truth at all. Nor am I saying that none of them are true. But the fact is that materialism and idealism cannot both be true in isolation of each other. The key lies in paradox. Chesterton says that in Christianity, paradox

> "separated… two ideas and then exaggerated them both. In one way Man was to be haughtier than he had ever been before; in another way, he was to be humbler than he had ever been before. In so far as I am Man I am the chief of creatures. In so far as I am a man I am the chief of sinners." Chesterton concludes: "Here, again, in short, Christianity got over the difficulty of combining furious opposites, by keeping them both, and keeping them both furious."

If your head is spinning as you are reading this, that's okay! You are not alone; this is heady stuff. Let me take Chesterton's courage example from above and put it more plainly here. If you do not care much about living and are willing to die, that requires no courage; therefore, courage dies. And if you care so much about your life that you are not willing to die, you will also kill courage. Courage requires both a love for life and a willingness to die, and that is the key to paradox. Both truths are needed. You need to love living, but you must also be willing to die—even be willing to die so that someone else can live. Once both are part of the equation, the tension and truth of courage are achieved and sustained. Chesterton also unlocks the power of paradox by encouraging us to exaggerate the truths in opposite directions. Watch what happens with courage. The more you love your life and the more you love living and the more you are willing to die and are ready to die for life and for others to live, the more your courage quotient grows.

Take Paul the Apostle as an example. He did not want to die; he was on a mission from God to spread the good news of the Gospel of Christ to as many people as possible. But this mission was dangerous; he almost died several times and eventually did die because of his mission. Paul knew people wanted to kill him because of the message he was spreading, and he kept spreading it in the face of death. Yet Paul is the one who coined the phrase "To live is Christ and to die is gain." He knew death was nothing to be feared, and heaven would be far better than his earthly existence; he knew God was in control of his life and death. Thus, he was not afraid to die; he was potentially even excited to die; he just did not want to die because he saw great purpose in his living. In light of this truth, one can see why he was so ferociously courageous! It disturbs me when people mock martyrs who die for what they believe, calling them into question for not leaving or running away. These people do not want to die; they are willing to die. They live with such hope and trust in their beliefs that they will turn those beliefs into courage in the face of death.

Let's examine what happens when we water down one of these truths or when we take one in isolation from the other paradoxical, balancing truth. If we do not think to go to heaven after dying is gain, then we will hold tightly to life on earth. We will try to pack as much into it as possible, and we will be focused on satisfying ourselves in the here and now; we may fill our lives with meaningless junk and wasted hours of apathy or triteness. We will also be terrified of dying and will avoid anything that could cause us suffering. Now let's take the opposite: if you only live for heaven and do not see the power of living here and now for Christ, you will lose your purpose and meaning for getting out of bed each day in a world of persecution, suffering, and pain. You will lose your reason for interacting with others on a personal, relational, and material level.

When both a hope for eternity and a purpose and love for life are held in paradox, though, the result is stunning. When we believe that after physical death we will still have eternal life in a world that includes no suffering and we also believe that our life in the here and now has great purpose, then we can live and even thrive in the middle of suffering; in fact, we will have the strength and hope and freedom to even step into the suffering of others. When we hold both truths in tension and healthy opposition, we find a vigor and purpose for life combined with a freedom and hope that rests in great reward and peace in eternal life after death. In the couplet that closes John Donne's poem "Death Be Not Proud," he speaks of the whimsy of paradox:

One short sleepe past, wee wake eternally,
And death shall be no more, death thou shalt die.

I will indulge one more paradox—the paradox of grace and works—to illustrate the necessity that both parts of the paradox must be life-giving. Let's deal with grace first. I am known for being a grace junkie. I am glad for that reputation. Now that I have tasted real grace, I am a fanatic: I teach it a lot, and I come on strong, bold, and unashamed. Over and over I proclaim the truth that we can do nothing to earn our salvation either before or after we have accepted salvation by grace. If we minimize grace and add any effort or works or a ritual like baptism or a spiritual gifting like speaking in tongues, it ceases to be grace.

I tell my students to hold their hands out, and I "drop" salvation by grace in their hands. Done. It is a gift. We do nothing to earn it. We can only receive it—and then it's ours. It needs to be this way. My friend Jack Burgess said that if you can't abuse it, it is not real grace. Thus, all of our works have been separated from our salvation. This is essentially WHY we are saved by grace: because it's all grace, no manipulation, behavior, attitude, fear, coercion, or anything of the like can be used to force or coerce us into receiving (or losing) our salvation. God in his infinite wisdom could have saved us by works or fear or command, but he chose grace because it makes our service and love freely given and it maintains our dignity. By saving us this way, our motivation to serve and love God is totally free and up to our discretion. In his letter to the Galatians, Paul is adamant about this. He firmly states: "It is for freedom that Christ has set us free. Stand firm, then, and do not let yourselves be burdened again by a yoke of slavery" (5:1). We can serve him or not serve him; our poor behavior, bad attitudes, or lack of intelligence or understanding will not negate our salvation; if it did, it would be our righteousness saving us, not Christ's. Kris Vallotton notes, "That would be self-righteousness."

But are we to do nothing for the God who has given us life and salvation? Far from it. Paul puts it mildly when he says our entire lives are to be living sacrifices unto God. I spend a good two weeks talking about grace in my class; I spend two months talking about how we are to use our gifts and talents to serve and love God and build His Kingdom here on earth as it is in heaven. God himself died for us to free us from death and sin. He offered himself as our righteousness as a pure gift. He forgives all our sins and imperfections. With a God who has done all that—and more—who are we to give him only half our effort? Wouldn't a natural response to all this be to give him all we are, all we have? This is where the paradox works its mysterious wonder. If we water down grace, we end up with only works and self-righteous behavior laced with fear and manipulation. And if we water down our works, there are so many consequences: we become apathetic to the God who saved us and made us and equipped us for good works; we miss out on our purpose; we serve only ourselves and in the process do ourselves a disservice because we were made to serve God freely. Both grace and works are needed and needed in the extreme! The more we understand God's amazing grace, the more we want to serve him freely, motivated purely by love. The more we willingly offer our lives in service to Him, the more we understand the freedom of his empowering grace.

If we water down either "side" (grace or works), we dip into heresy, and the truth is lost! I have seen churches overemphasize works and deemphasize grace and overemphasize grace and deemphasize works. The healthiest churches I have been a part of are grace junkies who freely and lovingly (and usually joyfully) work their butts off for Jesus and His Kingdom! This is a true, satisfying paradox. It is not a copout; it is necessary surrender. Both are true, and both are in tension with the other. The key is to hold onto the tension because when we try to resolve the tension of paradox, we lose the truth.

Not all paradoxes are satisfying, however. Some are very unsatisfying, and we need to be able to determine if a paradox satisfies or is simply meaningless, a never-ending vortex of thought. First, let me define what I mean by the word "satisfying." "Satisfying" does not mean it can be understood entirely; nor does it mean all tension and mystery are resolved; it merely means that it matches with our perceptions of reality in a satisfying way; it is helpful and trustworthy in regards to worldview. I trust the satisfying paradoxes; they are on my personal Trust List, but the unsatisfying are not; they are not worthy of my trust. For example, idealism has a paradox embedded within its answers to the question of what happens when you die. If you do not achieve oneness with The One Perfect Spiritual Ideal, such as Nirvana, you cease to exist (even with the idea of reincarnation, because you never reincarnate as the same person). Yet, if perchance you do achieve oneness with the One (who is not you), then you cease to exist because you only exist as the one, or you let go of self and achieve nirvana. Thus, the paradox is this: if you do not make it, you cease to exist, and if you make it, you cease to exist. The true Buddhists I've met have told me I am right on with this explanation, and they ask why I am not a Buddhist since I understand it so well. They tell me that the goal of Buddhism is to achieve nothingness. I tell them that that should not be too tough because in essence, aren't they nothing already? A nice quiet pause usually follows this, and then a mutual nod with some friendly smiles. We both understand each other.

A paradox of materialism asserts that we have a perception of free will, but we do not actually have free will. We have impressions of meaning, but life is absurd. We have a desire for morality, but that desire is a-moral and merely chemical impulses. We are aware of our existence, but our existence is not objectively measurable. Monism is similar in its hollow circularity: authentic pantheists (monists) will assert that good and evil exist based on your perceptions and preferences, yet, because good and evil are only perceptions, they are arbitrary and elusive and do not really exist. Pantheists will say you must wake up and achieve unity with God, but you must never forget that you already are God. The noblest truth of Hinduism is a paradox: "God dwells in me as me" ("I am that which I am looking for"). However, if God is me, and I am God, then I am simultaneously not me and God at the same time.

Although there are unsatisfying paradoxes, there are also satisfying ones—and these are life-giving! This is a mystery, but we gain some understanding when we look at the paradox who is Christ. Christ holds all of reality in beautiful tension, in paradox. One of the central mysteries has to do with the nature of reality, an idea we explored earlier in this text. We need Jesus to be fully God and fully man, fully spiritual and fully material. If you water down either of these realities, the essential truths are lost! But when our view of Christ encompasses and honors both spiritual and material reality, the truths from the four worldviews are found in one complete whole: Christ! In him all four "strips" of the painting are joined together: Idealism's truth of the spiritual world and the perfect, objective ideal; Materialism's truth of the physical world and the individualism and relativity of humans; Monism's truth of the unity and connectedness of all things; and Religious Theism's truth of the relational distinction between God and Man. All these truths are "held" in Christ. In him, all the lights of the chandelier are on. He is the "image, the picture, the definition" we need.

But how can this be? How can Christ be ALL?

I believe the answer is found in the Trinity, in the three persons of God. Christ revealed God to be a God with three persons: Father,

Son, and Spirit. This is the prime paradox of full reality: the three are one, are united, yet they are distinct. These three are in a never-ending relationship of love with each other that has no beginning and no end, in which there is "mutual giving and receiving." For this reason, God is love: active, expressive, constant love. Theologians call the relationships between the persons of the Trinity the perichoresis, and many picture the perichoresis as an ongoing, beautiful dance. This dance is the Trinity's expression of love, and love flows from it in the creation of all that is, material and spiritual. The stars, the moon, you, me, peace, mountains, trees, hope, joy, rivers, giraffes, angels, babies, roly-poly bugs, family: all has been created—is being created—out of love overflowing from a relationship of endless love. And what was created in love was kept close; it was loved continually.

What went wrong with this? If this is what prompted creation, if creation was in a continual relationship of love with its Creator and with each other, how is it so broken today? How did we get to this state?

One of the overflowing gifts from the perichoresis was free will. The image of dance helps us see the sense of this. Humanity was created with the choice to love—or not love; to stay in relationship—or leave it. To dance with God or not. Remember our tendency to declare our own god, a god whom we can control, a god whom we can fully understand because he's our creation, because we've made god small and ourselves big? Humanity as a species has generally rejected God, and the beautiful garden—in which all creation, humanity included, lived in perfect relationship with the Creator God—was ruined, and humans, separated from loving relationship with God, have been prone to create gods in their own image ever since. The God of Love holds his hand out inviting us to join in the dance of the Trinity on the dance floor of eternity, and we refuse. Ongoing and deepening division—between man and God; man and man; man and nature—has been the result ever since. The Trinity in and as the Fullness of reality dances on, and we stand by with our drinks and appetizer plate, watching, mocking, doubting, hiding in shame or fear, all in one way or another missing out.

Without a relationship with God, humanity lost sight of God's standards of perfect love, goodness, and truth. Even when humans did catch glimpses of these standards, they found themselves incapable of living by them. Humanity needed help, and God provided it. God provided God—in human form. Fully God, fully human, Christ came. He revealed to us the Father God we'd pushed away; he revealed the standard of perfect goodness and truth and love, and he met it; he disabled death and separation and sin with his own death and resurrection; he restored us to right standing with God; he shared his unifying Spirit with us; and, with all this completed, he extended his hand to us in an invitation to join the dance of God.

Earlier I suggested picking up Mere Christianity and reading book one, here is where I have my students put down this text and pick of Mere Christianity again, and this time they are to read and annotate book two, approximately another thirty pages. If you want or need more on the theology of why belief in Jesus, and not just belief in "God," is essential, this is a must for you. Those thirty pages contain some of Lewis's most famous and poignant prose.

In Jesus the Christ we have the fullness of all reality: material and spiritual, divine and human. In Christ, we have light and beauty and goodness and truth. In Christ, we have life—to the full. I close this section with a few more thoughts from the apostle Paul and a poem by Chesterton.

"For he has rescued us from the kingdom of darkness and transferred us into the Kingdom of his dear Son, who purchased our freedom and forgave our sins.
Christ is the visible image of the invisible God.
He existed before anything was created and is supreme over all creation,
for through him God created everything
in the heavenly realms and on earth.
He made the things we can see
and the things we can't see—
such as thrones, kingdoms, rulers, and authorities in the unseen world.
Everything was created through him and for him.
He existed before anything else,
and he holds all creation together.
Christ is also the head of the church,
which is his body.
He is the beginning,
supreme over all who rise from the dead.
So he is first in everything.
For God in all his fullness
was pleased to live in Christ,
and through him God reconciled
everything to himself.
He made peace with everything in heaven and on earth
by means of Christ's blood on the cross.
This includes you who were once far away from God. You were his enemies, separated from him by your evil thoughts and actions. Yet now he has reconciled you to himself through the death of Christ in his physical body. As a result, he has brought you into his own presence, and you are holy and blameless as you stand before him without a single fault."

Colossians 1:11-22

Gloria in Profundis
By G.K. Chesterton

There has fallen on earth for a token
A god too great for the sky.
He has burst out of all things and broken
The bounds of eternity:
Into time and the terminal land
He has strayed like a thief or a lover,
For the wine of the world brims over,
Its splendor is split on the sand.
Who is proud when the heavens are humble,
Who mounts if the mountains fall,
If the fixed stars topple and tumble
And a deluge of love drowns all-
Who rears up his head for a crown,
Who holds up his will for a warrant,
Who strives with the starry torrent,
When all that is good goes down?
For in dread of such falling and failing
The fallen angels fell
Inverted in insolence, scaling
The hanging mountain of hell:
But unmeasured of plummet and rod
Too deep for their sight to scan,
Outrushing the fall of man
Is the height of the fall of God.
Glory to God in the Lowest
The spout of the stars in spate-
Where thunderbolt thinks to be slowest
And the lightning fears to be late:
As men dive for sunken gem
Pursuing, we hunt and hound it,
The fallen star has found it
In the cavern of Bethlehem.

SECTION 5
THE WORD

CHAPTER 24
"CHORUS"

In the beginning the Word already existed.
The Word was with God,
and the Word was God.
He existed in the beginning with God.
God created everything through him,
and nothing was created except through him.
The Word gave life to everything that was created,
and his life brought light to everyone.
The light shines in the darkness,
and the darkness can never extinguish it.

God sent a man, John the Baptist, to tell about the light so that everyone might believe because of his testimony. John himself was not the light; he was simply a witness to tell about the light. The one who is the true light, who gives light to everyone, was coming into the world.

He came into the very world he created, but the world didn't recognize him. He came to his own people, and even they rejected him. But to all who believed him and accepted him, he gave the right to become children of God. They are reborn—not with a physical birth resulting from human passion or plan, but a birth that comes from God.

So the Word became human and made his home among us. He was full of unfailing love and faithfulness. And we have seen his glory, the glory of the Father's one and only Son.

John testified about him when he shouted to the crowds, "This is the one I was talking about when I said, 'Someone is coming after me who is far greater than I am, for he existed long before me.'"

CHAPTER 25
THE FULLNESS

The Treachery of Images is a painting by the Belgian surrealist painter, René Magritte. The picture shows a pipe. Below it, Magritte painted the words, "Ceci n'est pas une pipe," French for, "This is not a pipe."

I assert that for humans there is a similar treachery related to our interpretation of reality (and theology and doctrine, for that matter). The Truth is found in a Being, not in a list of trustworthy answers to big questions. The Truth is not found in a book about a person or even in the very words of that Being. The picture of a pipe is not a pipe; it is a picture.

We often interact with pictures of reality or stories about reality and assume we have encountered reality in them. But this is not the case: we have encountered a picture or a story of reality, and these may very well reveal some reality or truth to us, but these, in and of themselves, are not reality. C. S. Lewis put it like this in his indelible sermon, The Weight of Glory:

> "Wordsworth's expedient was to identify it with certain moments in his own past. But all this is a cheat. If Wordsworth had gone back to those moments in the past, he would not have found the thing itself, but only the reminder of it; what he remembered would turn out to be itself a remembering. The books or the music in which we thought the beauty was located will betray us if we trust to them; it was not in them, it only came through them, and what came through them was longing. These things—the beauty, the memory of our own past—are good images of what we really desire; but if they are mistaken for the thing itself they turn into dumb idols, breaking the hearts of their worshipers. For they are not the thing itself; they are only the scent of a flower we have not found, the echo of a tune we have not heard, news from a country we have never yet visited."

I have taught philosophy to high school students in a private school setting for over twenty years. As I share the four major worldviews in which we humans trust and then move hearts and minds towards a Christ-centered view of the world, I come back again and again to this concept penned by Lewis and to the opening quote by

Chesterton. As I teach my students that each worldview is but a portion of the Truth—though we trust in our worldview and hold to it as if it were the whole—I am convinced more and more deeply that even if we were able to piece together the true pieces of all the worldviews, even if all the strips of the painting were reunited and the lights of the chandelier were all turned on, we would have the tenets of Truth, the images of Reality—a picture or a shining of it—but not Truth and Reality itself. For the fullness of Truth and Reality is found only in the undivided Trinity embodied in The Christ. Christ said that if we follow him and his teachings, we will know the Truth and the Truth will make us free, but it is not our following or our believing the Truth—the right facts or premises or axioms—that sets us free. It is Christ Himself. "If the Son sets you free," Jesus said, referring to himself, "you will be free indeed." The Truth is a Person: the Triune Personhood of God found in the ideal spiritual reality of the Father; the material embodiment of the Son, Jesus the Christ; and the unifying, life-giving wholeness of the powerful Holy Spirit of God. The truth is God: a Triune, living, loving being; paradoxically One God and Three Persons at once; Prime Mystery and Prime Reality.

In a book written to the new church in the city of Colossae (in modern-day Turkey), the Apostle Paul warned his readers not to be deceived by weak philosophy, bad doctrine, and shallow hearsay. Then he delivered this statement: "For in Christ lives all the fullness of God in a human body. So you also are complete through your union with Christ, who is the head over every ruler and authority" (Colossians 2:9-10 NLT).

Jesus himself calls out the religious "bible believers" of his day when he draws this very distinct line; he says "You search the Scriptures because you think that in them you have eternal life; and it is they that bear witness about me, yet you refuse to come to me that you may have life." (John 5:39-40)

I have the Bible on my trust list. As I read through the New Testament, I find that one of the main messages, if not the main message, is a compelling invitation to trust that the person, Jesus, is the embodiment of The Truth; he is the Truth incarnate—in the flesh. He is the one who will help us understand what is Really Real, because He is Really Real.

I will never forget a particularly cogent conversation with Dave Seely, one of my favorite people. Dave is a lifelong pastor, mentor, friend, and surrogate father to many, including me. He has always represented to me the authenticity of a seeker and pilgrim on a journey—on the journey. Under a cathedral of massive oak trees and a canopy of diamond stars, next to a warm, embered campfire, with my little Livi Rose sleeping on my lap, he and I discussed how easy it is to miss these vital truths about Reality. Dave is graciously approaching the culmination of his journey as a shepherd for the church and wishes he'd had this perspective offered to him 50 years ago. I feel grateful to have stumbled upon it in my late 30s. As the fire burned down, we lingered on these questions: "When Jesus was kicking around in the dust in the Middle East 2,000 years ago, why did so many miss who he was—who he is? Why did we and why do we miss it? What is going on in our culture that causes so many Christians to miss this essential understanding of ultimate Reality, of what it really means to be a Christian?" We discussed possible answers to these big questions long into the night, and finally, we both rested on this famous line: "I once was blind, but now I see."

So many of us need to make the leap from trusting information about the truth to trusting the Truth Himself. We need to go from trusting a list of trustworthy statements about Reality to trusting the fullness of Reality.

This book is not an attempt to be the truth. It is meant to point to the Truth. Just like René Magritte said a picture of a pipe is not a pipe, the list of trustworthy truths is not the Truth. It is a list of truths about the Truth—the triune God: Father, Son, and Spirit. The list of trustworthy sayings can point you to the living Truth who is worthy of your trust. Even as the Apostle John was writing words about the Word Himself whom he knew personally, ate meals with, and loved, John knew his words were different than the Word himself. His words point to The Word who became flesh, who became the Son and dwelt a while among us and who is now seated at the right hand of the Father. John's words point to the Spirit, which dwelt in Jesus while he was on earth and which dwells in us. This is the Spirit Jesus promised us before he returned to the Father. What else would give us life and life to the full but the life-giving Spirit of God dwelling in each of us, not as us, but distinct from us and making us more and more "us" while simultaneously shaping us into the image of our Loving Creator?

CHAPTER 26
THE HUG

"Imagine yourself as a living house. God comes in to rebuild that house. At first, perhaps, you can understand what He is doing. He is getting the drains right and stopping the leaks in the roof and so on; you knew that those jobs needed doing and so you are not surprised. But presently He starts knocking the house about in a way that hurts abominably and does not seem to make any sense. What on earth is He up to? The explanation is that He is building quite a different house from the one you thought of—throwing out a new wing here, putting on an extra floor there, running up towers, making courtyards. You thought you were being made into a decent little cottage: but He is building a palace. He intends to come and live in it Himself."

C. S. Lewis, Mere Christianity

"The very credentials these people are waving around as something special, I'm tearing up and throwing out with the trash—along with everything else I used to take credit for. And why? Because of Christ. Yes, all the things I once thought were so important are gone from my life. Compared to the high privilege of knowing Christ Jesus as my Master, firsthand, everything I once thought I had going for me is insignificant—dog dung. I've dumped it all in the trash so that I could embrace Christ and be embraced by him. I didn't want some petty, inferior brand of righteousness that comes from keeping a list of rules when I could get the robust kind that comes from trusting Christ— God's righteousness."

Philippians 3:7-9 MSG

The Fullness of Christ and Reality

The Lewis quote above brings us back to this book's purpose for using philosophy as a tool: it is not so we can engage in heady, wordy conversation—no! We have used philosophy as a practical tool to break down our understandings of Reality, to examine our worldview. And we have done this with an even greater purpose in mind: to piece our worldview back together with a greater understanding of it, with a greater understanding of what we believe in, what we trust in, what shapes our lives. I would like to re-emphasize another aim of this book: that we do this with grace, with love, and with honor. These elements allow us to break down, examine, and rebuild our worldviews—and, more importantly, to pursue Truth, The Living Truth,—in authentic, healthy, life-giving community.

This book thus far has, I hope, helped you construct a philosophical dwelling place, a worldview home built of that which is trustworthy. My worldview, as you well know by now, is based on trust in Christ, and though I wrote the previous acts in this book to readers with varying worldviews, that changes at this point. The rest of this book is written to readers who want to become Christ-Centered Theists more fully or to live more intentionally as such or who simply have open minds to learn more about my limited perspective on this issue. I now deliberately point you to the life and message of Jesus—to Jesus Himself—with the hope you will invite (or get to know better) the Living Truth into the house you have built or are building. The truth is not the house that you used the hammer of philosophy to build, nor is it the trustworthy axioms and reliable trust lists you are utilizing. The Truth is a Person you get to invite to live in your house with you. The Truth is the "pneuma," the life-giving breath of God that already by his grace and love gives life and being to all his beloved creation. The Truth, the Apostle Paul says, is not far from each of us, and this same Truth—this Person!—who brought the universe into being came to earth two thousand years ago as a human and ate fish on a beach with his friends. He is the Author of Life and of the Great Story that encompasses all of us, and he is, amazingly, very eager to communicate with each of us about the smaller stories we find ourselves in—and eager to invite us to join him in the creating of them! His ears are attuned to our hearts, and His Pen is in Hand.

The four trust lists used in this book point us to a person, to the person of Christ, to the Truth as the Living, Incarnate, Fullness of Reality. Philosophy in this book is used as a tool, a means to an end—and that end is Christ; however, as mentioned earlier in this book, the intention is not to use apologetics to ruin other people's words, worlds, views, or worldviews. The approach I am suggesting is more about addition than it is about subtraction. Though partial truths can be very destructive and demolition of partial and complete untruths is an integral part of rebuilding, at some point we have to build; we have to construct. This requires trust, but the wonderful thing is that the Holy Spirit of Christ is an expert at creative, rebuilding work. The Lewis quote at the beginning of this chapter gives us a powerful image of how God's rebuilding of our selves—through difficult and sometimes painful—is a loving "process."

Moving from Metaphors to Christ Himself

Our ultimate aim in this book (and, I would argue, in life) is to discover and eventually love and intimately know that you are loved by Christ, but, now, paradoxically, we must return for a while to the very metaphors we used earlier to lead us to Him. First, we established this truth: a "strip" of Christ's garment is still a piece of Christ's garment! It contains truth! Ironically, in John 19:23-24, John gives us the detail that Christ's cloak was divided into four parts. I'm not sure why John pointed out this detail—other than the fact that John is a poet, and poets know details are essential—but for the purposes of this book's approach to worldview, I want to lean into this detail. Christ's cloak, symbolizing his whole, undivided person, is split into four parts and we are clinging to our single strips as if it is the whole—as if it is the fullness itself.

Let's review another metaphor. Remember our use of the painting The Last Supper by Leonardo da Vinci? I described the horror of such a work of art being parceled into four sections, but I noted that a piece of the painting is still a piece of the masterpiece, a part of the original. We can and must honor it as a piece of the Truth. We then talked about discovering the truth each piece contains as well as the gaps that have been filled in. Next, we talked about Christ as the fullness of reality, the entire painting, the chandelier fully ablaze with light.

And here's where this can be unsettling. When we encounter the full, real person of Christ, it is difficult to know how to look back on our old worldview. On my own journey, I had to come to the excruciating realization that I had kept a painting of Jesus on the wall of my worldview house and I had assumed it was the real thing. Upon my coming to know the living Triune God, the Christ who reveals the Triune God, I felt horrified by the illusion of an illusion I had formerly clung to. I didn't know what to do with it at first. I had to learn how to surrender my former hold on that strip of reality, on my partial understandings and limited information. I knew if I didn't let go, the consequences could be tragic and profound. I knew this because I was already seeing the collateral damage in my life and close relationships all around me.

I hope that whatever strip of the Truth you cling to will ultimately point you to, even lead you to, the Truth Himself. It can and should if you surrender it, if you stop clinging to the idea that it must be the full truth. And when you bring your rent rags to Jesus—all those partial truths—may you find that the truth you cling to is made complete only in Him. You will not be disappointed but will instead be astounded by the depth of the truth you were already holding—how it is made fuller and alive in Him! You may find that you simply drop what you are holding in order to hold onto or be held by Him.

In a story in the Gospel of John, the powerful Roman official Pilate is faced with Truth. The arrested Jesus is standing in front of him, and Pilate asks the famous question: "What is truth?" (John 18:38). The Roman quest for truth was for an abstract concept, a set of ideas, the right string of words. Pilate wanted a definition of truth, like something a dictionary or internet or library search could give you. However, The Truth is a Being, The Being, The Living God—and it was standing right in front of him! John says the "Logos"—the Prime Reality—became Flesh. The truth was incarnate: "in–carne"—in the flesh. The Truth was right in front of Pilate; he could see Jesus, touch Jesus, hear Jesus! In chapter 14, verse 6 John records Jesus saying, "I am the Way and the Truth and the Life." He does not say he will simply teach about the truth or write it down, or show people where to find it. He says He is it.

An Invitation to Life, as Seen in The Great Divorce

C. S. Lewis captures this concept brilliantly in his book The Great Divorce, which, like The Screwtape Letters, requires some mental adjustments when reading. In Screwtape, the reader has to understand that when the "enemy" is mentioned, it is God being referred to. In The Great Divorce, it is easy to miss the main themes and general context due to the style of the text (dream literature). Many readers do not understand the connection to the allegory of the cave nor the "Shadowlands" references that create the context for all the dialogue and opening chapters of The Great Divorce. The entire book is set as a dream and an "imaginative supposal"—it is the classic "I wonder what would happen if…" situation. I insert this book into my course later in the semester because the entire story is about encountering the Whole of Prime Reality as the Kingdom of God.

My introduction to The Great Divorce in my classes goes something like this: "Imagine if there were a group of people living in darkness and shadow—separated from their true identity, from Prime Reality, separated from God and Full Life, separated from the Kingdom of God. Call it Hell if you wish… that's what it will eventually be if they remain there forever. Imagine if Jesus were to take a big golden Bus, his Magic Bus (cue the song…) into this land filled with shadows and darkness. Imagine if Jesus filled this bus with "shadow people" and then drove this busload of shadows to the edge of his Kingdom of Light and Life, a Solid country that is Really Real, not a shadow of reality. Imagine if there were Solid People, Kingdom People, People solid in their faith, identity, and being, living in the Kingdom. Imagine if these Kingdom people had conversations with the shadows and invited them to stay…"

When we understand what C. S. Lewis is doing in The Great Divorce (and it usually takes at least until chapter 4), we can then enter into the story and identify with the characters as they decide if they will say yes to Joy, Freedom, Hope, and Life; if they will say yes to Prime Reality; if they will surrender their "no" and say "yes" to The Kingdom. This decision requires both a "no" and a "yes." A simple "yes" is not enough. When they accept the invitation to enter the Kingdom of Light and Life, they are also saying "no" to the land of the shadows. Only then can they stay in the Kingdom and learn wholeheartedly to walk, then run, then dance… This entire story ends up being an invitation to Joy, an invitation to Life, an invitation into Being, from shadow to Substance. The quest for Truth is, truly, an invitation. To me, this is pure "evangelism." This is all evangelism really is, and maybe all it needs to be: an invitation to "Real Joy," an invitation to the Kingdom, a call to meet the King Himself.

Thus—returning to the book—imagine if all these shadows had the chance to stay in the Kingdom. What would they do? Sadly, Lewis pens conversation after conversation of people who choose to go back to the land of Shadow. They choose to remain in darkness. They decide to remain in the cave. They, like Pilate, reject the Truth right in front of them. They reject God, Life, and Life Abundant. When we enter the story of The Great Divorce, we notice it is not God who does the rejecting; it is the shadow characters who reject God.

All Great Stories point to the True Great Story, the one we are in. The Great Divorce is one of them. The genius of this book is that a careful reading allows insight into the potential motivations of those who reject The Kingdom of God. Though I find the truths in this book sometimes cause me pain, it is one of my favorite books. I have read it at least once a year for the past twenty years. I have taught it twice a year for at least 15.

Before we look at a few passages from the book, here is a final insight: it helps to imagine that the entire book takes place on earth—not in heaven and hell. Think of the entire setting as earth and the two places in the story as the Kingdom of God and the Kingdom of Shadows. Remember that Jesus repeatedly says the Kingdom of God is "at hand," "near you," upon you," and "within you." We can step into the Dominion of the King at any moment. Jesus says, "He who has eyes, let him see, he who has ears, let him hear."

This reminds me of the moment in The Great Divorce when the shadows first arrive at the Kingdom. It is a threshold moment of pure, gracious invitation to life and joy. One of the shadows is talking to the Jesus character, the Driver of the Bus.

"'Hi, Mister,' said the Big Man, addressing the Driver, 'when have we got to be back?'

'You need never come back unless you want to,' he replied. 'Stay as long as you please.' There was an awkward pause."

I love that awkward pause, and I fear it. After this quote, I take the students in my class to the middle of the text. The story is told by a narrator who is in the story itself. This narrator has observed the shadows and shared each one's choices regarding the land of shadows and the kingdom of light. The tension has built as readers have understood that the narrator has not yet made a choice for himself. He asks his guide, George MacDonald, a poignant question that is one of the hinges of the entire text.

"'But what of the poor Ghosts who never get into the omnibus at all?'

'Everyone who wishes it does. Never fear. There are only two kinds of people in the end: those who say to God, "Thy will be done," and those to whom God says, in the end, "Thy will be done." All that are in Hell, choose it. Without that self-choice there could be no Hell. No soul that seriously and constantly desires joy will ever miss it. Those who seek find. To those who knock it is opened.'"

The Shadow's Choice is Ours: Pilate or Mary?

In light of this scene, contrast Pilate's encounter with Christ (described above) with Mary's encounter with Christ just after he is resurrected (John 20:16-18). Mary was a seeker, even to the point of seeking out the dead body of Jesus. Planning to mourn his death, she is instead amazed at his Life. I love this story, but I must admit I am also a little jealous. Anyone who knows me knows I am a hugger, so when I read this passage and imagine Mary privileged to give the first hug to the risen savior—her risen savior!—I get a small twinge of envy.

Mary literally, physically hugs the TRUTH—and then she becomes the first evangelist! That might be the perfect recipe for evangelism!

This is the concept of "Perichoresis" embodied in Jesus, opened up to us by Jesus. The Trinity is perpetually inviting all of us, the Beloved, into the Divine Dance of God's Love.

As you read and process this text, you may be trusting in a piece of the truth and not the Truth itself. You may also not really understand what this means. Let's go back to Chesterton's metaphor of the silly strips of torn cloth; the point is we ultimately need to get beyond the clothing and the tunic to the Being Himself. This book is just clothing. The trust lists are just His garments. The seamless cloak is an excellent metaphor for the person of Christ, but ultimately we must set aside trust list items and ideas and individual truths (however good they are) and even truths from all the trust lists pulled together and instead cling to Jesus himself! For some of us, that relationship might start with our crawling through the dust to His feet, just as another Gospel account narrates Mary doing (enacted in the movie The Passion of the Christ).

For others, the relationship may be more like the beautiful but awkward hug Mary gives Jesus in the account recorded in John's Gospel. I love that hug. It is a physical act, involving the body as well as the mind; it reveals she is interacting with a person!—not information, not a sacred scroll, not the Bible, not a story, not a trust list or a worldview or a philosophy or a doctrine or theology about Jesus. It is Mary hugging a living, breathing, human being: Jesus.

Of course, people who are clinging tightly to a section of the garment of the fabric of reality, people like you and me, will often claim with fervor, "I do not have a piece of reality. What I have is the Truth, and I have it all figured out." I used to say this often, but then I realized I was repeating it every time I gained new insight, thinking my new view was complete. Clearly, I had not had it all figured out before, nor would my new insight complete my worldview. I now lose trust in anybody who declares, "I have it all figured out."

Paradoxically, those who arrogantly claim with the utmost certainty that they are right are often the ones who have the hardest time letting go of the "silly strip" they are clutching and learning to embrace other aspects of truth. It is often tough for them to accept the living, breathing, fullness of Reality found in the Trinity. I know this painful truth from personal experience. Unfortunately, many people are content clinging to the clothing, unlike Mary. Here's the account:

Now Mary stood outside the tomb crying. As she wept, she bent over to look into the tomb and saw two angels in white, seated where Jesus' body had been, one at the head and the other at the foot.

They asked her, "Woman, why are you crying?"

“They have taken my Lord away,” she said, “and I don’t know where they have put him.” At this, she turned around and saw Jesus standing there, but she did not realize that it was Jesus.
He asked her, “Woman, why are you crying? Who is it you are looking for?”
Thinking he was the gardener, she said, “Sir, if you have carried him away, tell me where you have put him, and I will get him.”
Jesus said to her, “Mary.”
She turned toward him and cried out in Aramaic, “Rabboni!” (which means “Teacher”).
Jesus said, “Do not hold on to me, for I have not yet ascended to the Father. Go instead to my brothers and tell them, ‘I am ascending to my Father and your Father, to my God and your God.’”
Mary Magdalene went to the disciples with the news: “I have seen the Lord!” And she told them that he had said these things to her.” (John 20:11-18)

Grace Enables the Hug

Mary's relationship with Jesus was utterly by grace. His grace to her—and to us—is a gift. It is grace that helps us trust him, to understand he sees and knows us; grace that we can believe him and hope in him; grace that allows us to surrender to him. Our relationship with Jesus is not dependent upon the depth of our emotions or the strength of our hugs; it is not dependent on the strength of our clinging to him. Yet, as can be seen in another story about Jesus's clothing, even a tiny pinch grip on the "hem of (Jesus') robe" can deepen our relationship with and trust in him.
Just then a woman who had been subject to bleeding for twelve years came up behind him (Jesus) and touched the edge of his cloak. She said to herself, “If I only touch his cloak, I will be healed.”
Jesus turned and saw her. “Take heart, daughter,” he said, “your faith has healed you.” And the woman was healed at that moment. (Matthew 9:20-22)
When we finally arrive at clasping the Real Being himself in our own way and in our own time, this Savior, Friend, and King, the living Truth Himself, will probably respond to each of us in the same way he did to the woman who courageously touched the hem of his robe or to Mary in the Garden in that moment of powerful

embrace. We might find Him saying something like (this is the NMT: New Matthew Translation), "Stop clinging to me; stop clutching me; stop hugging me so tightly. Enough with the bear hug. I love hugs, I really do, but let me see your beloved face. Let us walk together and talk. I have more to give you than simply a hug." We often stop at salvation by faith and grace, and we miss His loving face and embrace. We miss the deep relationship and intimate companionship that are the natural progression and outworking of that salvation.

Choosing to Be Overwhelmed by Grace

When I first moved from mere adherence to a list of faith statements to being overwhelmed by Jesus himself, I wondered, "What will I do when I move past the verbiage and finiteness of language and words into relational connection with the living God of the universe?" You may be wondering the same. What happens when we move past simple salvation into grace-full relationship? As in any relationship, this takes risk and trust. I am confident that when you encounter the Real Being Himself, you will not be disappointed. If you are disappointed, it was not God. I believe this encounter is ultimately what we are all longing for; it's what we were made for. And when I say all, I mean all. I believe every human being on the planet is longing for that extended hand and loving glance, longing for that invitation to dance with God. In the story of Jesus, and thus Christianity, this is essentially what we have been invited into.

If this is what you want, then this book, like a compass, is meant to point you towards Him. It is not intended to simply give you more words about Him. If you want to interact with fabric, metaphors, or paintings, you may find the pages of this book interesting, but you will have missed the entire point. You will have the picture of a pipe and not a real pipe. You will have words but not The Word. You will have the invitation to the dance but miss out on The Dance itself.

If you are waiting for me to tell you what the Dance will be like for you, you will have to keep waiting, for how could I presume to tell you what your Divine Dance with Love will be like? This is the Love who created you, who knows you inside and out, who knows you better than you know yourself—it will be a Dance perfectly suited for who you are. You need to take the step for yourself and say yes to the Invitation. I can assure you that you will not regret it, and it is precisely what you are yearning, longing, and hoping for. Jump into it with both feet. Or dive in! Once you jump or dive, you can't go back to where you started; it is a free fall. Cling tightly around Jesus. I'm assuming you have hugged someone who has something in their hands: a book, coffee, a phone, a computer. I have received and even given hugs with stuff in both my hands—the so-called chin hug—but what I love about real hugs is that you need to drop what's in your hands (even this book) and wrap your arms around the being in front of you. And if it's God, don't ever let go!

In other words, this book is simply an invitation to the greatest party, the best relationship, the fullest life, the best way to live. Get to know a person, The Person. I end this long section with a few more poignant words from Jesus; these are the words I put in the opening pages of this text.

"I am praying not only for these disciples but also for all who will ever believe in me through their message. I pray that they will all be one, just as you and I are one—as you are in me, Father, and I am in you. And may they be in us so that the world will believe you sent me.

"I have given them the glory you gave me, so they may be one as we are one. I am in them and you are in me. May they experience such perfect unity that the world will know that you sent me and that you love them as much as you love me. Father, I want these whom you have given me to be with me where I am. Then they can see all the glory you gave me because you loved me even before the world began!

"O righteous Father, the world doesn't know you, but I do; and these disciples know you sent me. I have revealed you to them, and I will continue to do so. Then your love for me will be in them, and I will be in them."

John 17:1-5 & 13-26 (NLT)

CHAPTER 27
THE ENCOUNTER

The Day a Modern-Day Pilate Visited My Class

One of the most remarkable moments of my teaching career happened a few years ago when we had a delightful, world-renowned atheist visit our class as a guest. We all had a great time; he was consummately kind and honoring, engaging and insightful. Several of my 100-plus students said it was one of their most memorable days of all of high school. This very intelligent scholar, prolific writer, and talented speaker walked us through his perspective on the atheist answers to the seven questions in this book. He overwhelmingly approved of the verbiage set down here and made light of a few of the nuances of my wordings. For example, after reading my materialist answer to "What is a human being?" he stated, "You make me sound like I am a sack of chemicals—which I guess is accurate but not very sexy." (You may recall I included his description earlier.)

Additionally, he confirmed one of my teachings by unwittingly mimicking it exactly. For over ten years, when I got to the question about meaning and purpose for authentic materialism, I would simply turn to the whiteboard and write "WHY" and then grab a red marker and draw a circle around the word and a line through it. Then I would say, "For the authentic atheist there is no 'why.' Humans simply 'are.'" It was apropos when he literally did the exact same thing: when he arrived at the last question, he wrote "WHY" in capital letters, grabbed the red marker, circled it, and added a strikethrough. He then followed my quote with word-for-word accuracy. I was pleasantly stunned, as was he when I revealed to him what had just happened.

There were two indelible marks from that day for me. The first was when I asked him if there were any questions he would prefer me not to ask in front of the students. He said he would greatly appreciate if I spared him any questions on free will and human autonomy. Fair enough—but this certainly gave me something to think about! The most powerful moment came at the end of the day from an unprompted yet invited question. A caring, genuine student asked what it would take for him to convert to believing in Jesus. His reply was magnificent. He said that it would not be another attempt at evangelism, nor another Bible verse. (He had already shared that he, like most sincere atheists, has studied the Bible profusely and read it several times cover to cover.) Surprisingly he said a wondrous sign from God or a miracle in front of his face would not do it either. He had witnessed a number of those already. I pressed him on this, asking if he would be convinced if the student with the broken leg sitting in the front row in class was instantly healed right there in front of everybody. "Nope," he said, "I have already seen that sort of thing. The only thing that will truly do it for me is a loving, powerful, undeniable, personal encounter from a personal God who knows my name and wants an authentic, real, loving relationship with me." Silence filled the room. The bell rang. I remember the look of solidarity on so many of the students' faces.

Needless to say, the next day's class proved to be very fruitful. We discussed the immense power of the "encounter" moment juxtaposed with the many faithful who have never had an "encounter" but are still confident they are saved by grace through their faith in Jesus, the Immanuel. The moment of epiphany settled into the room and lingered all day like the fragrance of fresh flowers or incense in a cathedral. In regards to our guest the day before, it was as if we'd all been transported through time to witness the moment when a powerful, well-educated Roman ruler asked the most critical question of the day and yet missed his encounter, missed his answer. Pilate had a literal, physical encounter and conversation with God and did not realize it! He did not, could not, and would not recognize God as God, Jesus as the Truth, and a Person as Prime Reality. Pilate not only missed the encounter, but he also gave permission for the torture and destruction of the Truth.

We had the privilege to see a similar scene enacted right in front of us. It was the Shakespearian Act 4 "twist" moment at its highest (and lowest). Our new Atheist friend knows an encounter is what will transform his heart and mind, will convert his soul and save him from the Shadowlands, yet because of his fractured worldview, he will not recognize God when this encounter happens. He has not accepted Jesus for who he is, God Incarnate, and has, like the Pharisees did, labeled him as demon-possessed or misguided, and rejected the Truth of who he is. I saw this realization on the faces of my students; one by one they got it.

They understood the whole point of studying all the worldview stuff. It most definitely did not have anything to do with grades and memorizing lists of information... They realized that if we do not have an honest, accurate view of who God really is and what True Reality is, we will miss it when it is right in front of us. Has this clicked for you yet?

One or two students glowed with an inner light that literally leaked out of their pores. They knew Jesus because, they had met him; they knew God and were holding his hand right there in class while other students had merely seen his picture on the walls of their lives or the screens of their phones. Many of my students had to settle into the fact that they had missed their encounters like they had missed meeting their favorite celebrity sitting at a nearby restaurant table all night. I was reminded of the scene in Scripture when the Pharisees, trying to make Jesus slip up and say something that they could use against him, brought to him a woman caught in adultery. They kept yelling at Jesus and picked up stones to kill the woman, but when Jesus knelt and began writing in the dirt with his finger, they, one by one, went silent, dropped their stones - their hearts - and left. Faced with the presence and reality of Jesus, they chose to leave rather than to acknowledge who he is, rather than to get personal with him. The woman encountered him; she saw him for who he was, and she let him see her for who she was, but the Pharisees didn't (John 8:1-11). I saw this acted out in my class that day, the day my students realized that each of them, like my atheist friend, was faced with a choice regarding Jesus, and that choice affected everything. We sat in silence. No one spoke. No one moved. I put on some quiet music, and we sat in graceful contemplation until the bell called us back to my classroom and the rest of the day.

Jesus All Around Us: Facing Our Choice

C.S. Lewis wrote many letters to many people. In one to a friend named Malcolm, he wrote: "We may ignore, but we can nowhere evade, the presence of God. The world is crowded with him. He walks everywhere incognito. And the incognito is not always hard to penetrate. The real labor is to remember, to attend. In fact, to come awake. Still more, to remain awake." (Letters to Malcolm: Chiefly on prayer, Chapter 14, Para. 11, p.75.) In this letter, Lewis was echoing King David in Psalm 139, in which David, a former shepherd, mused, "I can never escape from your spirit! I can never get away from your Presence!" (verses 7&8). I am sure David learned this in his shepherding days in the quiet countryside. As David stayed close to his sheep, watching over them as they walked the rolling hills, singing over them to settle them, fighting lions and bears to protect them, he learned God's Spirit was doing the same with him, always communing with him, ever present.

My students and I realized this truth—of God's constant, abiding, quiet presence—when we invited a friendly, honest, intelligent atheist into our lives. We had a good conversation filled with love, laughter, honor, honesty, candor and a genuine pursuit of Truth. We recycled our agendas and put down our swords, got out the comfy chairs and hot drinks and had a conversation. I have come to believe that conversations like this can change the world, at least my world.

Jesus said that when you seek, you will find. (Matthew 7:7-8) And in the Old Testament the prophet Jeremiah speaks on behalf of God when he says to the people of Israel "If you look for me wholeheartedly, you will find me. I will be found by you," says the Lord." (Jeremiah 29:13&14a) For you and me, I think this means that we need to figure out who God is so that when we see him, we don't miss him. The character of George MacDonald in the Great Divorce says to the narrator in the heat of one of the central discussions in the story "Never fear.... No soul that seriously and constantly desires joy will ever miss it. Those who seek find. To those who knock it is opened." I think this also means on our individual journeys we need to keep seeking and surrendering and submitting until we encounter the Real Truth Himself.

Ironically and painfully much of this reminds me of the unique situation that the Dwarves are in at the ending of The Last Battle in the Narnia series by Lewis. These dwarves are sitting in a beautiful green field next to the kings and queens of Narnia end even Aslan himself, yet they see it as dark, the food is rank, and the ground is uncomfortable. Here is a taste of that passage.

> "You see," said Aslan. "They will not let us help them. They have chosen cunning instead of belief. Their prison is only in their own minds, yet they are in that prison; and so afraid of being taken in that they cannot be taken out. But come, children. I have other work to do." (186).

Jesus' name is Immanuel, God with us. He is in us and with us and all around us. The encounter is not something far away or rare. Even before Jesus came to earth, as I mentioned earlier, David knew the immanence of God. He wrote: "Where can I go from your presence?" and he answers his own question, in beautiful poetic fashion, with an emphatic, "Nowhere!" Jesus says the Kingdom of God is in the midst of us. If the King's Dominion is with you, then the King Himself must have access there as well. Scripture includes picture after picture of God walking with people: with Adam and Eve in the garden, with Enoch, with Noah, with Abraham, with the disciples, with the two on the road to Emmaus. This invitation to "walk with" was not just extended to people whose names ended up in Scripture. It was recorded in Scripture to let us know this invitation is extended to all of us.
Luke is very clear when he writes that the Holy Spirit was not just for those in the upper room or a small elite group of the original apostles. He connects the fresh outpouring with the prophet Joel's declaration years before.

"Then, after doing all those things,
I will pour out my Spirit upon all people.
Your sons and daughters will prophesy.
Your old men will dream dreams,
and your young men will see visions.
In those days I will pour out my Spirit
even on servants—men and women alike.
And I will cause wonders in the heavens and on the earth—

This passage says "on all people" not "a small group of isolated, perfect people who are elitist, ego-driven and get it all right, especially their theology and doctrine..." No way! The apostle John says; "God so loved THE WORLD that he gave his Son." At the Birth of Christ Luke records: "That night there were shepherds staying in the fields nearby, guarding their flocks of sheep. Suddenly, an angel of the Lord appeared among them, and the radiance of the Lord's glory surrounded them. They were terrified, but the angel reassured them. "Don't be afraid!" he said. "I bring you good news that will bring great joy to ALL PEOPLE. The Savior—yes, the Messiah, the Lord—has been born today in Bethlehem, the city of David! And you will recognize him by this sign: You will find a baby wrapped snugly in strips of cloth, lying in a manger."

Suddenly, the angel was joined by a vast host of others—the armies of heaven—praising God and saying,

"Glory to God in highest heaven, and peace on earth to those with whom God is pleased."

Scripture uses another picture to show us how intimate God wants our relationship with him to be. We are told in several places and in several ways we are the new Temple of God: our hearts and our bodies can literally be the "most holy place" on the planet, the place where God dwells! Paul's tone is almost rhetorical when he addresses the saints in Corinth: 'Don't you realize that your body is the temple of the Holy Spirit, who lives in you and was given to you by God?' (1 Corinthians 6:19)

When we do not enter into this relationship of intimacy with God, we also miss intimacy with other people. But the opposite is also true: genuine relationship with God leads to more authentic relationship with others! This is what true religion is meant to lead to. Healthy, vibrant, life-giving religion is intended to be an excellent tool that leads to loving, honoring relationship. If it does not—or if it not used in this way, with this aim in mind—it is like a faulty map or bad directions. Jesus did not come to start a new religion; he came to fulfill one! He came, in many respects, to reinvent traditional religion altogether. He came in a body in part to show us how we, in bodies ourselves, can have a relationship with God and each other.

Looking for, but Not Controlling, the Encounter

The old, dead, dry, rule-following, morally correct, politically correct, religiously correct, "religious spirit" in me screams at myself and judges myself for putting in a poem with the word "fat" and for choosing a Sufi Mystic as my poet. (All the more reason to keep it in here at this point of this section.) Every time I read this poem, it makes me smile, and it reminds me of the disciples with Jesus, who must have laughed so much on all their crazy escapades and capers. I want to laugh with Jesus on my journey with Him. C. S. Lewis says, "Joy is the serious business of Heaven." My soul says yes to that!

Before I end this chapter, I want to make it clear that I am fully aware we cannot and must not fabricate or manufacture the "God encounter moment" for people—or even for ourselves; yet the God-encounter moment is what often marks full surrender on our personal journeys of faith. In The Lion, The Witch, and The Wardrobe, Tumnus the fawn famously muses about the Jesus-like lion named Aslan. "He'll be coming and going," Tumnus says. "One day you'll see him and another you won't. He doesn't like being tied down—and of course, he has other countries to attend to. It's quite all right. He'll often drop in. Only you mustn't press him. He's wild, you know. Not like a tame lion."

We cannot manufacture our encounters with God or demand them, but at the same time, it is hard to miss the encounter moment if we have eyes to see and ears to hear. When Christ is in all things and through all things and in the holding-together of all things, then He is ever-present, omnipresent, immanent. Read all the encounter moments shared in Scripture. See the irony: often while one person meets God, others right next to them miss it.

Encounter Moments in Narnia

These encounter moments often changed the trajectory of a person's entire life. C. S. Lewis included many such encounter moments in his Narnia stories. They are potent scenes, for when characters meet Aslan face to face, they are changed. In the book Prince Caspian, there is a scene in which Lucy and her brothers and sister have gotten lost. After a day of wandering, they have finally gone to sleep in a forest. Lucy wakes in the middle of the night and connects with Aslan. But one of the most telling moments is the next morning when Lucy is the only one who can see him and the other children can't.

For the readers who are familiar with The Chronicles of Narnia by Lewis, you may want to take some time to ponder the transformative power of each individual encounter throughout the Narnia stories. If you have never read the Narnia tales, here is your official invitation.

- How is one moment different from another?
- What does each moment say about the concept of each of the characters in those stories being on an individual Journey? And what does it say about Aslan's Timing for each Individual Character?
- In the Horse and His Boy How does Aslan's Quote to Shasta "Child,' said the Lion, 'I am telling you your story, not hers. No

one is told any story but their own." reflect our need for a grace-filled and trusting understanding of God and His timing for individual encounters on each of our Journeys?

- Find some more examples in Narnia: Start with Eustace and Aslan when Eustace is a Dragon; Edmund and Aslan after Edmund's Time with the White Witch; Lucy's ability to see Aslan when the others cannot see him...

Encounter Moments in Scripture

Again, you may want to take some time to read and reflect on the unique personal touch in the following Jesus Encounter Moments in the Bible. How does the concept of Perichoresis fit these passages?

-Moses' request not to go on without the presence of God
-A Conversation with the woman at the well in John 4
-Dignity for the woman caught in adultery in John 8
-A Conversation with Nicodemus in John 3
-Dinner with Zacchaeus in Luke 19
-Personal touch with Malcus' and his ear in John 18
-Peter's numerous Encounters (google them...)
-John resting his head on the shoulder of the Truth at Dinner in John 13
-Thomas and Jesus in John 20
-The Walk with Jesus to Emmaus in Luke 24
-Pentecost! In the opening chapters of the Book of Act
-Philip and the Ethiopian's Encounter in Acts 8
-Paul's Divine Encounter in Acts 9

Your Invitation to Encounter and Beyond

In this book I have given you several invitations: first was the invitation to listen to the views of others, to dialogue; next was the invitation to examine your trust list and your worldview, to tear it apart for the purpose of rebuilding it; third, I invited you to look at truths both in and outside your own worldview and to bring the pieces of truth together to see more clearly the fullness of reality; the greatest invitation came next: to see Jesus as the fullness of reality—the complete painting, the blazing chandelier—and to embrace him fully. Now comes the final invitation: to journey with Jesus. It's an invitation that comes straight from Jesus himself. He promises to never leave you on this journey. He promises to guide you and walk with you. He says He is for you, entirely for you.

CHAPTER 28
THE POWER OF LOVE

""Look! I stand at the door and knock. If you hear my voice and open the door, I will come in, and we will share a meal together as friends." Revelation 3:20

"It would seem that Our Lord finds our desires not too strong, but too weak. We are half-hearted creatures, fooling about with drink and sex and ambition when infinite joy is offered us, like an ignorant child who wants to go on making mud pies in a slum because he cannot imagine what is meant by the offer of a holiday at the sea. We are far too easily pleased." C.S. The Lewis Weight of Glory

The Truman Show is a movie about a man who was born and raised on a television set created to resemble a small town. This man, Truman, grew up on this set and does not realize he lives in a make-believe world, entertaining all who watch. The house he lives in and the water he sits by are all part of the set, as are the relationships he has with his family and his friends. Nothing in Truman's world is authentic, and he begins, bit by bit, to realize this. In a scene near the end of the movie, Truman is on a boat clutching the picture of a girl who represents authentic love and genuine relationship. She is the only one who ever tried to tell Truman the truth about his "reality." Truman has decided he will do anything it takes to get out of his cave of deception and manipulation to meet this real girl. The director, not wanting Truman to escape and end the show, manufactures a storm to keep Truman's boat from reaching the end of the make-believe world. Yet, Truman has an inkling that there is a life worth pursuing beyond this false reality wherein he can find real people who offer real love. Into the raging storm, Truman yells, "You are going to have to kill me!" A feat the director is unwilling to accomplish. Truman, or rather True-Man, knows it is worth dying for real love. Life without real love is not a fulfilling life but merely a shadow of a fulfilled life. Truman risks it all to break free from the entrapment of shadows. And rather than losing his life, he is freed to finally begin living it. He finds real love.

Have you?

Will you?

A Few Words On Love and Intimacy

What if the ultimate goal on our human journey is not just about reaching a destination like Heaven or the Kingdom of God? What if these destinations, or even the journey to these destinations, are simply spaces for the creation of something even greater? What if the ultimate goal of this entire journey is to love God and receive His love for you? Being in the Garden of Eden was not the main point of the opening of the Story. Eden was a setting which supported the growth of intimacy between Adam and God, one man and His Creator. Thankfully, growing intimacy between God and His creation was not limited to that setting. Today, in a world filled with other people, you can experience God's divine love as if you are the only person on the planet, as if you and God were the only ones on the planet. You can receive His love for you and allow it to shape your perspective of self. His love teaches us how to love self. And in turn, that understanding of how to love self releases us into a position of being able to love others. Out of the fullness that is created from God's focused love for you and only you, you can offer love to others without interruption of the fulfillment of your own need for love. Christ, your first source of love or your 'first love,' will never run out of what you need. This supply of love is unending as you stay connected to Him, as you abide in Him. In several instances, Jesus refers to this endless supply as a "river" that flows into us, fills us, and then flows out from us. And from that fullness, you can start loving others as God has fully loved you - extravagantly, outrageously, completely, eternally. You can finally "love your neighbor as you love yourself."

Earlier in this text, one of the most personal questions that humans face was examined regarding the pursuit of the meaning and purpose of existence. For this text, I have phrased it as thus: Why are we here? Where are we going? What is the purpose of human existence? To be or not to be? What is the purpose of living for tomorrow? I have come to trust, with all of my being, that we are created for the intimacy of a loving relationship. Outside of intimacy, we remain in a position of searching. In the preface of his book, "Eager to Love," Richard Rohr highlights the importance of intimate oneness with God.

> "Bonaventure echoed that understanding of unique and intimate vocation when he taught, 'We are each loved by God in a particular and incomparable way, as in the case of a bride and bridegroom.' Francis and Clare knew that

> the love God has for each soul is unique and made to order, which is why any "saved" person always feels beloved, chosen, and even "God's favorite" like so many in the Bible. Divine intimacy is always and precisely particular and made to order—and thus "intimate" (4).

Our need for intimacy is found and filled in more than the physical realm. Matter matters but so does the spiritual. Jesus says that man cannot live on "bread alone." He acknowledges that we have needs, and those needs are diverse. Physical foods meet the needs of the physical body, just as spiritual food will meet the cravings and needs of the spirit. We cannot use the material things in our lives, the physical parts of our world, to meet the needs of the spiritual. Many of the "sins" we struggle with are due to trying to use something physical to meet our real spiritual needs. Food, drugs, and sex cannot meet our spiritual need for intimacy in an authentic and lasting way. The inverse can also be true: if we substitute the spiritual for the material, we find a similar negative vortex. Intimacy with God does not negate our need for intimacy with humans. And it is out of our intimacy with God we can authentically connect with and love others.

Marriage is not a pre-requisite to or a guarantee for finding intimacy. Ironically, some of the people I know who are most free and fulfilled, most confident in Christ and their own identities, and most intimate with God are unmarried. St. Bonaventure, St. Clare, St. Francis, Mother Theresa, and Richard Rohr did not connect their lives in a marriage covenant to another human being yet lived fulfilled. Even C. S. Lewis was single for most of his life; he married Joy Davidman when he was 45 years old, and Joy died four years later. Lewis recognized his identity in Christ before he married, and therefore, he did not expect his spouse to solely meet his need for intimacy, a need which is only wholly met in relationship with Christ. He reflects on this truth in Book Two of Mere Christianity when he is musing about free will. He says,

> "The happiness which God designs for His higher creatures is the happiness of being freely, voluntarily united to Him and to each other in an ecstasy of love and delight compared with which the most rapturous love between a man and a woman on this earth is mere milk and water. "

Ultimately, our ability to intimately connect with God is influenced by our willingness to trust critical truths: God is good, and He is Love itself, we are saved by grace, we are no longer condemned as Christ took all of our punishment upon himself on the cross, we are God's beloved children (implying that Jesus is our older brother and that God truly is our Father), nothing can separate us from the unconditional love of God that is in Christ Jesus, and we are sealed for the day of redemption. Living in the reality of these truths redefines our purpose, freeing us to love self and others rather than hobble along, shackled by fear, obligation, guilt, or shame. Using divine love as a motivation and guide to robustly live is the culmination of this entire text, and it is the starting point for the rest of the journey. We are not adequately prepared to follow Jesus as authentic disciples until we have actualized His love for us. In turn, this releases us to fulfill the King's new command, "love one another." As authentic disciples of Jesus, we are to be "known by our love." As Jesus said, "So now I am giving you a new commandment: Love each other. Just as I have loved you, you should love each other. Your love for one another will prove to the world that you are my disciples." John 13:34-35. And to Jesus, love is the substance of the top two commandments: 'Jesus replied, "'You must love the Lord your God with all your heart, all your soul, and all your mind.' (Deut. 6:5). This is the first and greatest commandment. A second is equally important: 'Love your neighbor as yourself.' (Lev. 19:18). The entire law and all the demands of the prophets are based on these two commandments.'" Matthew 22:37-40. (NLT)

Paul also emphasizes the unifying power of love in his letters to the new saints in Corinth who are debating theological flashpoints. Paul poignantly states: "'Now regarding your question about food that has been offered to idols. Yes, we know that "we all have knowledge" about this issue. But while knowledge makes us feel important, it is love that strengthens the church. Anyone who claims to know all the answers doesn't really know very much. But the person who loves God is the one whom God recognizes' (1 Corinthians 8:1-3). In the renowned passage from 1 Corinthians chapter 13, Paul teaches that even if we are supernaturally charged believers, without love we are nothing and our efforts amount to clanging cymbals – noise at best. I have viscerally experienced that those who claim to follow Christ but do so without love are not simply "nothing" or "noise," but they are often spiritually destructive and abusive. He also deliberately and carefully notes that love is greater than faith and hope and that love never fails us! It is worth a deliberate pause and reflection when someone with Paul's authority testifies that something is greater than that which saves us: Faith.

Love is more than important; love is vital, it is essential, and in the truest meaning of that word, it is the "essence" of the message and the calling.

John, the disciple, uniquely calls himself the "one that Jesus loved." An attentive reading of his writings reveals that John was intimately loved by Jesus, and he knew it. Ironically, we are all intimately loved by Jesus; I wonder how many of us know it. John knew this truth so well that he wrote about it, making it his identity and legacy. I wonder how many of us have yet even to receive His Life-giving love? John beautifully and powerfully teaches about this love in I John, chapter four.

'Dear friends, let us continue to love one another, for love comes from God. Anyone who loves is a child of God and knows God. But anyone who does not love does not know God, for God is love. God showed how much he loved us by sending his one and only Son into the world so that we might have eternal life through him. This is real love—not that we loved God, but that he loved us and sent his Son as a sacrifice to take away our sins. Dear friends, since God loved us that much, we surely ought to love each other. No one has ever seen God. But if we love each other, God lives in us, and his love is brought to full expression in us. And God has given us his Spirit as proof that we live in him and he in us. Furthermore, we have seen with our own eyes and now testify that the Father sent his Son to be the Savior of the world. All who declare that Jesus is the Son of God have God living in them, and they live in God. We know how much God loves us, and we have put our trust in his love. ***God is love, and all who live in love live in God, and God lives in them.*** *And as we live in God, our love grows more perfect. So we will not be afraid on the day of judgment, but we can face him with confidence because we live like Jesus here in this world. Such love has no fear because perfect love expels all fear. If we are afraid, it is for fear of punishment, and this shows that we have not fully experienced his perfect love. We love each other because he loved us first.' 1 John 4:7-19 (NLT)*

CHAPTER 29
I MUST FOLLOW

Many blessings to you on your quest for the Truth. The final word for my classes and for you is simply to remember that we are on a journey, each of us. The journeys of literature and history teach us that they are not straight paths with mile markers regularly spaced along the way. They are instead filled with trials and triumphs, sorrows and joys, despair and hope. We must remember that everyone else is on a journey, too, and we are all at different places and stages of this journey that is unique for each of us. How can you lovingly help someone move to the next stage of his or her journey? How can you equip or empower someone with courage to take one more step? This is an essential component of a loving community. We can honor the process of each person's individual journey. We can love each other, love self, and extend grace to all. We can have confidence and enduring hope that the King has come, His Kingdom is coming, and His Kingdom has no end.

You shall go out in joy and be led forth in peace; the mountains and hills will burst into song before you, and all the trees of the field will clap their hands.

Isaiah 55:12 (NIV)

When I think of all this, I fall to my knees and pray to the Father, the Creator of everything in heaven and on earth. I pray that from his glorious, unlimited resources he will empower you with inner strength through his Spirit. Then Christ will make his home in your hearts as you trust in him. Your roots will grow down into God's love and keep you strong. And may you have the power to understand, as all God's people should, how wide, how long, how high, and how deep his love is. May you experience the love of Christ, though it is too great to understand fully. Then you will be made complete with all the fullness of life and power that comes from God.

Now all glory to God, who is able, through his mighty power at work within us, to accomplish infinitely more than we might ask or think. Glory to him in the church and in Christ Jesus through all generations forever and ever! Amen.

Paul in his letter to the Church in Ephesus 3:14-21 (NLT)

WORKS CITED & SELECTIVE BIBLIOGRAPHY

Augustine of Hippo, "On Christian Doctrine," in Readings in Medieval History, edited by Patrick J. Geary, second edition, 28-46, (Peterborough, Ont.: Broadview Press, 1997), pp. 32-33.

Berry, Wendell. Collected Poems: 1957-1982. New York: North Point Press, 1984.

Berry, Wendell. The Country of Marriage. Berkeley, CA: Counterpoint, 2013.

Blavatsky, H. P. The Key to Theosophy. Wheaton, IL: Quest Books, 1972.

Boethius. The Consolation of Philosophy. Translated by Richard Green. New York: Macmillan, 1962.

Brother Lawrence. The Practice of the Presence of God with Spiritual Maxims. Grand Rapids, MI: Spire Books, 1994.

Brown, William. "World of Worldview." The Torch. Cedarville University, 2004.

Camus, Albert. The Stranger. Trans. by Matthew Ward. New York: Vintage International, 1989.

Carpenter, Humphrey Ed. The Letters of J. R. R. Tolkien: with assistance of Christopher Tolkien. Boston: Houghton Mifflin, 1981.

Carroll, Lewis. Through the Looking-Glass and What Alice Found There. 1871. Oxford: Oxford University Press, 1982.

Chesterton, G.K. Collected Works. San Francisco: Ignatius Press, 1986.

———. The Everlasting Man. San Francisco: Ignatius Press, 1993.

———. Orthodoxy. Wheaton: Harold Shaw Publishers, 1994.

Campbell, Joseph. From Petty, Anne C., One Ring to Bind Them All Tolkien's Mythology. University of Alabama, 1979.

———. The Power of Myth. New York: Anchor Books, 1988.

———. The Hero With A Thousand Faces. 3rd Ed. Novato California: New World Library, 2008.

Dawkins, Richard. The Selfish Gene. Oxford. Oxford University Press. 2006.

Dawkins, Richard. The God Delusion. New York: Mariner Books, 2006.

Dickson, John. A Doubter's Guide to the Bible: Inside History's Best Seller for Believers and Skeptics. Grand Rapids, MI: Zondervan, 2014.

Duncan Entertainment. The Magic Never Ends: The Life and Work of C.S. Lewis, Documentary. 2001.

Glyer, Diana. The Company They Keep: C. S. Lewis and J. R. R. Tolkien as Writers in Community. Kent Ohio: Kent State University Press, 2007.

Glyer, Diana. Bandersnatch: C.S. Lewis, J.R.R. Tolkien, and the Creative Collaboration of the Inklings. Kent Ohio: Black Squirrel Books, 2015.

Goff, Bob. Love Does: Discover a Secretly Incredible Life in an Ordinary World. Nashville: Thomas Nelson, 2012.

Hafiz. The Gift: Poems By Hafiz the great Sufi Master. Trans by Daniel Ladinski. New York: Penguin Compass, 1999.

Harris, Sam. Free Will. New York: Free Press, 2012

Harris, Sam. Letter to a Christian Nation. New York: Random House, 2006.

Harris, Sam. The End of Faith: Religion, Terror, and the Future of Reason. New York: W. W. Norton, 2004.

Heidegger, Martin. Being and Time. Trans. John Macquarrie & Edward Robinson. San Francisco, CA: Harper & Row, 1962.

Heschel, Abraham Joshua. The Sabbath: Its Meaning for Modern Man. New York: Farrar, Straus, and Giroux, 1951.

Hitchens, Christopher. God Is Not Great: How Religion Poisons Everything. New York: Twelve, 2007.

Kilby, Clyde S. The Arts and the Christian Imagination: Essays on Art, Literature, and Aesthetics. Brewster, Massachusetts: Paraclete Press, 2016.

Kilby, Clyde S. Images of Salvation in the Fiction of C. S. Lewis. Wheaton, Il: Harold Shaw, 1978.

Knight, Gareth. The Magical World of the Inklings: J. R. R. Tolkien, C. S. Lewis, Charles Williams, Owen Barfield. Longmead, England: Element Books, 1990.
Koenig, H. G. Religion, Spirituality, and Health. Adv Mind Body Med. 2015 Summer; 29(3):19-26.

L'Engle, Madeline. Walking on Water. New York: Convergent Books, 1980.

Lewis, C. S. The Chronicles of Narnia. One Volume Edition. New York: HarperCollins, 2001.

———. Collected Letters. Ed. Walter Hooper. 1 vol. London: HarperCollins, 2000–2006.

———. Collected Letters. Ed Walter Hooper. 2 vols. To date. London: Harper Collins, 2000-2006.

———. Collected Letters. Ed. Walter Hooper. 3 vol. London: HarperCollins, 2000–2006.

———. The Collected Poems of C. S. Lewis. Ed. Walter Hooper. London: Fount-HarperCollins, 1994.

———. The Discarded Image: An Introduction to Medieval and Renaissance Literature. 1964. Cambridge: Cambridge University Press, 1967.

———. English Literature in the Sixteenth Century, Excluding Drama. 1954. Oxford History of English Literature 3. Oxford: Oxford University Press, 1973.

———. An Experiment in Criticism. 1961. Cambridge: Cambridge University Press, 1988.

———. The Four Loves. 1960. San Diego: Harvest-Harcourt, 1988.

———. God in The Dock: Essays on Theology and Ethics. Grand Rapids, Michigan: William B. Eerdmans Publishing Company, 1970.

———. The Great Divorce. New York: HarperCollins, 2001.

———. Letters to Malcolm: Chiefly on Prayer. New York: Harcourt Brace and World, 1964.

———. The Lion, the Witch, and the Wardrobe. 1950. New York: Harper Trophy-HarperCollins, 1994.

———. The Magician's Nephew. New York: Macmillan, 1955.

———. Mere Christianity. New York: HarperCollins, 2001.

———. Miracles. New York: HarperCollins, 2001.

———. "Myth Became Fact." C.S. Lewis Essay Collection: Faith, Christianity, and the Church. Ed. Lesley Walmsley. London: HarperCollins, 2002.

———. The Pilgrim's Regress. Grand Rapids, MI: Eerdman's, 1981.

———. The Screwtape Letters: with Screwtape Proposes a Toast. 1942; 1961. New York: HarperSanFrancisco-HarperCollins, 2001.

———. Surprised by Joy: The Shape of My Early Life. New York: Harcourt, Brace and World, 1955.

———. That Hideous Strength: A Modern Fairy-Tale for Grown-Ups. 1946. New York: Collier-Macmillan, 1965.

———. Till We Have Faces: A Myth Retold. 1956. New York: Harcourt Brace, 1985.

———. The Weight of Glory and Other Addresses. 1949. Grand Rapids, MI: Eerdmans, 1979.

Lewis, Warren Hamilton. Brothers and Friends: The Diaries of Major Warren Hamilton Lewis. Ed. and Intr. Clyde S. Kilby and Marjorie Lamp Mead. San Francisco: Harper and Row, 1982.

Lloyd-Jones, Sally. The Jesus Story Book Bible: Every Story Whispers His Name. Grand Rapids MI: Zondervan, 2007.

Lloyd-Jones, Sally. Thoughts That Make Your Heart Sing. Grand Rapids MI: Zondervan. 2012.

Love Poems from God: Twelve Sacred Voices from East and West. Translated by Daniel Ladinski. New York, Penguin Group, 2002.

Lunsford, Andrea A. and John J. Ruszkiewicz, Editors. The Presence of Others: Voices and Images That Call For Response. 3rd Ed. Boston: Bedford St. Martins, 2000.

MacCullough, Martha E. Undivided: Developing a Worldview Approach to Biblical Integration. Colorado Springs, CO: Purposeful Design, 2016.

Martindale, Wayne, and Jerry Root Editors. The Quotable Lewis. Wheaton IL: Tyndale House, 1990.

McKee, Robert. Story: Substance, Structure, Style, and the Principles of Screenwriting. New York: HarperCollins, 1997.

Merton, Thomas, New Seeds of Contemplation. New York, New Direction, 2007.

Nietzsche, Friedrich. The Madman. Translated by David Chase, 2010. (Used with permission)

Nietzsche, Friedrich. Thus Spoke Zarathustra: Ed. By Adrian Del Caro and Robert Pippin. New York: Cambridge University Press, 2006.

Nouwen, Henri J. M. Life of the Beloved: Spiritual Living in a Secular World. New York: Crossroad, 2015.

Nouwen, Henri J. M. The Return of the Prodigal Son: a Story of Homecoming. New York: Image Books, 1994.

Ortberg, John. If You Want to Walk on Water, You've Got To Get Out of the Boat. Grand Rapids MI: Zondervan, 2001.

Penninga, Mike. "God, I Have a Question…Part 2 Don't All Roads Lead to You?" Kelowna Gospel Fellowship Church. April 2013. Web. www.kgfchurch.com

The Republic of Plato. Translated by Allen Bloom. New York: Basic Books, 1968.

The Qur'an. Trans. M.A.S. Abdel Haleem. New York: Oxford University Press, 2015.

Rohr, Richard. Adam's Return: The Five Promises of Male Initiation. New York: Crossroad. 2016.

———. Creating Christian Community. 2009.

———. Eager To Love. Cincinnati Ohio: Franciscan Media, 2014.

———. Falling Upward. San Francisco: Jossey-Bass, 2011.

———. Immortal Diamond: Searching for our True Self. San Francisco: Jossey-Bass, 2013.

Rota, Michael. "Why You Can Still Bet your Life on Christ: An Updated Version of Pascal's Wager Offers a Powerful Argument for Christian Commitment." Christianity Today, 24 April 2016.

Silk, Danny. Culture of Honor, Destiny Image, 2009.

Sire, James. The Universe Next Door. Downers Grove: InterVarsity Press, 2009.

Tolkien, J. R. R. "Beowulf: The Monsters and the Critics." 1936. The Monsters and the Critics and Other Essays. 5–48.

———. The Hobbit: or There and Back Again. Foreword. Christopher Tolkien. Special 50th Anniversary Ed. 1987. Boston: Houghton Mifflin, 1966.

———. The Letters of J. R. R. Tolkien. Ed. Humphrey Carpenter with the assistance of Christopher Tolkien. Boston: Houghton Mifflin, 2000.

———. The Lord of the Rings. One Volume Edition. Boston: Houghton Mifflin, 1994.

———. The Monsters and the Critics and Other Essays. Ed. Christopher Tolkien. London: HarperCollins, 2006.

———. "Mythopoeia." Tree and Leaf. Boston: Houghton-Mifflin, 1965. 97-101

———. "On Fairy Stories." Tree and Leaf. Boston: Houghton-Mifflin, 1965. 9-73

———. The Silmarillion. Ed. Christopher Tolkien. Boston: Houghton Mifflin, 1977.

———, trans. Sir Gawain and the Green Knight, Pearl, and Sir Orfeo. Ed. and Preface. Christopher Tolkien. Boston: Houghton Mifflin, 1975.

———. Tree and Leaf Including the poem Mythopoeia. 1964. Intr. Christopher Tolkien. Boston: Houghton Mifflin, 1989.

Tozer, A. W. The Knowledge of the Holy. New York: Harper Collins, 1961.

Tzu, Lao. Tao Te Ching: Interpreted as Nature and Intelligence by Archie J. Bahm. Albuquerque, NM: World Books, 1986.

VanderLaan, Ray. In the Dust of the Rabbi: That the World May Know. Grand Rapids: Zondervan, 2009.

Walmsley, William Ed. C. S. Lewis Essay Collection and Other Short Stories. Great Britain: HarperCollins, 2000.

Williams, Charles. The Place of the Lion. 1931. Grand Rapids, MI: Eerdmans, 1980.

'Trust in the Lord with all your heart; do not depend on your own understanding.'

Proverbs 3:5

'"But blessed are those who trust in the Lord and have made the Lord their hope and confidence. They are like trees planted along a riverbank, with roots that reach deep into the water. Such trees are not bothered by the heat or worried by long months of drought. Their leaves stay green, and they never stop producing fruit.'

Jeremiah 17:7-8